The
Borina Family
of Watsonville

by Mike Wallace

MUSEUM OF ART AND HISTORY @ THE MCPHERSON CENTER

SANTA CRUZ, CALIFORNIA

Printed in Canada

First printing — December 2013

————————

Excerpts from the oral histories, *Mary Ann Borina Radovich: Croatian Apple Farmer, Watsonville, California, 1918-1977*; and *Ray Travers: Three Generations of Apple Farming in Watsonville, California, 1875-1977*, both conducted by Meri Knaster, are reprinted with permission from the Regional History Project of the University Library at the University of California, Santa Cruz. See http://library.ucsc.edu/reg-hist/ for the complete transcripts of these oral history interviews.

Photographs on pages 74 and 87 used courtesy of Covello & Covello photography, 831.423.2922.

————————

Library of Congress Cataloging-in-Publication Data

Wallace, Mike (Michael Eugene), 1950-
The Borina family of Watsonville / by Mike Wallace.
     pages cm
Includes bibliographical references and index.
ISBN 0-940283-24-7
1. Borina, Nick, 1889-1949. 2. Secondo, Lucy, 1888-1941.
3. Borina, Nick, 1889-1949–Family. 4. Croatian Americans–
California–Watsonville–Biography. 5. Immigrants–California–
Watsonville–Biography. 6. Watsonville (Calif.)–Biography.
7. Watsonville (Calif.)–Genealogy. 8. Watsonville (Calif.)–Emigration
and immigration–History. 9. Dalmatia (Croatia)–Emigration and
immigration–History. 10. Apple industry–California–Watsonville–
History. I. Title.
  F869.W28W35 2013
  929.20973–dc23
                    2013038835

This book is dedicated to the memory of

June Borina Schnacke

in honor of her love of her family and
her concern for the people and land of the Pajaro Valley.

Contents

Foreword

IF YOU LOOK CLOSELY at the dark, rich soil of the Pajaro Valley, you can see the threads that make up the tapestry of immigrant groups who turned the valley into one of the richest and most diverse agricultural engines in all of California. Some of those threads are better known, and can be followed back across the Pacific to Asia (China, Japan, the Philippines) or southward to Latin America (Mexico, El Salvador) or eastward across the Atlantic to Europe (Ireland, the Azores, Denmark).

One thick but less well known strand in the valley's history stretches back to the rugged eastern coast of the Adriatic, beginning in a region that has come to signify confusion and complexity: the Balkans. Almost from their first arrival in the 1880s, immigrants from this area hid behind general misunderstandings about who they really were. Their invented group name became "Slavonians," though in truth they were really Croatians within various political entities from the Austro-Hungarian Empire to Yugoslavia. It was just easier to say Slavonian when asked, "Who are you people?" than to give the more accurate history lesson.

The Croatian story in the Pajaro Valley is tightly woven and convoluted, in part because of a native reluctance to talk about themselves and also because the story is just flat-out complicated. The two Croatian sisters, Donna Mekis and Kathy Mekis Miller, brilliantly chronicled the big picture in the first-ever examination of the Croatian story, *Blossoms into Gold: The Croatians in the Pajaro Valley*.

Now Mike Wallace gives us the first detailed chronicle of one of the most influential Croatian immigrant families. Using his considerable journalistic skills and an amazing command of the family's personal and public records, Wallace lays out a story worthy of a Hollywood movie. In some ways, the saga of the Borinas fits the template of the typical Croatian immigrants. Nick Borina, the family patriarch, arrived in the Pajaro Valley with nothing but his wits and drive (and wearing mismatched shoes), and through hard work and determination was able to build a family business that weathered bad times and good.

But there's much more to the story than immigrant makes good. The Borina story has many twists and turns, tragedies and triumphs, and Wallace tells it against the backdrop of the entire twentieth century, from the effects of the 1906 earthquake to the major events in Santa Cruz County's history.

It is the Borina women who occupy the story's heart; Nick's wife, Lucy, and their two daughters, Mary Ann and June. The two daughters were the first female Pajaro Valley-born Croatians to graduate from Stanford University (1940), but there's more. June Borina went on to get a law degree from Stanford and become Santa Cruz County's (and California's) first female district attorney, while Mary Ann applied her considerable managerial skills to running the Borina family business following the death of her parents.

Most immigrant success stories would end with the succeeding generations reaping the rewards of the work of their parents and grandparents, dissolving to the image of a large family reunion of the lucky descendants, who would either live happily ever after or would take the family fortune to ruin in conflict and bickering.

Not the Borina story. There were no descendants. There was no third generation to inherit the fruits of the fierce determination of

Nick and Lucy Borina and their talented daughters. And this is where the Borina story takes another turn: June Borina decided to give the family fortune back to the Pajaro Valley, where it was created.

In the book's final chapter, Wallace describes how June, in her will, brought together her goddaughter, Sheila McLaughlin Burke, and her trusted family attorney, Bill Locke-Paddon as founding trustees of what came to be the Borina Foundation. Together they set up a foundation that would not only help disperse future earnings from family properties but also would protect the many farmers who had spent their lives working the rich valley soil. Since its establishment in 2002, the Borina Foundation has already given millions of dollars to charitable and educational projects in the Pajaro Valley.

The Croatians left many monuments to their successes scattered across the valley, and the living generations continue to provide the respect and honor for their founding members. The Borina Foundation has assured that the legacies of Nick, Lucy, Mary Ann and June will also be honored and remembered. In a real sense, all of the residents of the Pajaro Valley are now the Borina extended family, enjoying the fruits of the hard work and vision of those first two generations. This book will ensure that all who read it will know and understand how this happened.

The Borina family may have come to an end with June's death in 2000, but the Borina Foundation will guarantee that the family name lives on forever. This story should become a part of the basic tapestry of the Pajaro Valley. Thanks to Mike Wallace's masterful telling, it will.

—Sandy Lydon,
     Historian Emeritus, Cabrillo College, Aptos, California

Preface

FROM 1887 TO 1924, there was a mass migration from the Dalmatian coast of what is today Croatia to the California farm town of Watsonville, about 90 miles south of San Francisco. Land holdings in the old country were typically small and could support only one adult child, usually the eldest son and presumptive heir. In most cases, the other male children were essentially pressured to find work elsewhere, and many came to coastal California. These energetic young immigrants brought to the Watsonville area an understanding of land and farming, a keen sense of business, and an ethic of hard work and frugality. Collectively, they turned the apple orchards of Watsonville and the surrounding Pajaro Valley into an economic powerhouse. Individually, a number of them built foundations of enduring wealth; it's estimated that a third of the farm land in the Pajaro Valley today is owned by families of Croatian descent.

The story of the great migration and growth of the Pajaro Valley apple industry was finally unearthed and beautifully told by Donna F. Mekis and Kathryn Mekis Miller in their 2009 book *Blossoms into Gold: The Croatians in the Pajaro Valley*. But that larger story is composed of hundreds, if not thousands, of individual stories that make up the mosaic. This book is an attempt to look at one extraordinary family, the Borinas, whose lives had a profound influence — in terms of agriculture, politics and philanthropy — on the Pajaro Valley and beyond.

It's a story that spans the 20th century, beginning in September of 1900 when 11-year-old Nick Borina arrived at Ellis Island in New York. In one sense it ends with the death of June, the younger daughter and last remaining family member, in 2000. Yet in another sense the family legacy continues today and will continue for centuries to come, largely owing to June's vision and the steps she took to bring it to fruition in the last years of her life.

By all accounts, the Borinas — every one of them — were tough, shrewd and hard-working. They were a close-knit family that produced two daughters who were ahead of their time in doing work that had traditionally been the province of men. One daughter took over the family farming operations and steadily improved them while adjusting to the demands of a changing agricultural marketplace. The other went to law school and became the first female district attorney in the state of California at the age of 27. And that's only part of the family saga.

The Borina family history is not without the ordinary amount of conflict, controversy, sorrow and family dissension, but in the end this is a story about family values — in particular, a respect for hard work and education; a love of the land and farming; and of giving back to the community. With the family gone and those who knew them diminishing in numbers, that story had been slowly disappearing with each passing year. This book is an attempt to tell as much of it as possible from the available record as a way of showing what they did and the difference that one family can make in a community.

Nick Borina. Patriarch of the family, he was nearly broke when he rode a bicycle into Watsonville, wearing a pair of mismatching shoes. Twenty years later, he was one of the biggest apple growers and packers in the region — some say the biggest.

⌐○⌐

Chapter 1

Nick Borina

Niko Borina, who came to be known as Nick, was born December 20, 1889, in Osojnik, about five miles north of Dubrovnik on the Dalmatian coast of the Adriatic, which was then part of Austria. Niko, named after a grandfather, was the second surviving son in a family of eight children, six of whom lived to adulthood (another son, born before Nick, died at the age of six months and was also named Niko, after the grandfather). Osojnik was a hardscrabble farming town, with a population of about 600. Owing to those circumstances, one fundamental fact of his future was all but determined at birth: He would likely leave and seek his fortune elsewhere, and perhaps at a very early age.

"Being next to the oldest means that you have to leave home," his daughter Mary Ann said in a 1977 UC-Santa Cruz oral history interview. "You leave the area there and go live with some other family somewhere else to work ... immigrate ... or, whatever alternative was open you'd have to take it because only the oldest son stayed at home." Most of the men who left were able to send money back home, and many hoped to return at some point, but it was an uncertain future, and while the oldest son generally stayed in the old country, a number of oldest sons in that area did emigrate to America.

At the time of Niko's birth the Borinas had been living in Osojnik for more than a century, having moved there in the late 1700s from a

Nick Borina's beginnings. Born in Osojnik (above), one of many small and poor farming towns near the Dalmatian coast, Nick spent his early years in a small stone house (below) that was home to his parents and six children. Photos: 2004.

village about 25 miles to the north. The family name, an uncommon one, was taken from the nickname of an ancestor, Petar Filipović (1678-1741). Petar was known as Bore, possibly related, for reasons unknown, to the first names Borislav or Boroje, which somewhere along the way morphed into Borina.[1] There are no Borinas left in Osojnik now, just as there are no Borinas left in Watsonville.

Details of young Niko's early life in Croatia are unrecorded and forgotten, aside from the recollection that he helped his farming family by tending sheep. But the hard realities driving many younger sons to

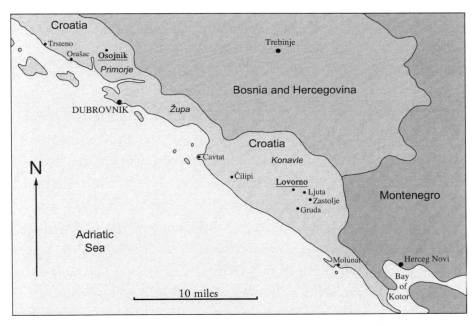

Southern Croatia. Borinas came from Osojnik (upper left) and Secondos came from Lovorno (middle right). Part of Croatia today, when Nick Borina was born it was part of the Austrian Empire. Dubrovnik, the largest city in this area, has a population of around 50,000.

leave the family home and earn money elsewhere must have been felt by the family. As laid out by the Mekis sisters in *Blossoms into Gold*, the pressures that made a family farm unsustainable for more than one off-spring included high taxes, population growth owing to health improvements, and crop failures. All young men faced the prospect of mandatory military service, and the maritime industry, which in bygone days had offered jobs that were an alternative to farming, was shrinking. Given all those factors, it was not surprising that some parts of Croatia saw 10 percent of the local population emigrate in a single year.[2]

In the late summer of 1900, Niko's parents, Mato and Marija, sent him to America. He was not quite 11 at the time, and traveled with a group of countrymen from Dubrovnik to Le Havre in France, where they left for New York on the steamship *La Bretagne*, arriving September 10. From there he crossed the United States by train, ending up in San Francisco, where an aunt who lived at 2004 Fillmore Street had vouched for him and would take him in. Several people from his area of Dalmatia came over on the same boat, and three of the women went on to San Francisco, so Niko was not entirely alone,[3] but it was nonetheless a long and dramatic journey for a child his age.

"He came here to his uncle in San Francisco, who had a restaurant," his daughter Mary Ann later recalled in the oral history interview. "The job that was open to him there was washing dishes, and he said he saw enough dishes to last his whole life. He gave that up after a few years. He wasn't interested in that. He just didn't like any indoor job."

Young Nick worked days at the restaurant in San Francisco and went to school at night for six or seven years, learning English and the basics of the three R's. He also grew to be a tall, strong man. His citizenship papers later describe him as standing five feet, eleven and a half inches, weighing 225 pounds, and having black hair with grayish eyes.

San Francisco's great earthquake and fire of 1906 gave Nick a chance to move on from dishwashing. Rebuilding the city afterward required plenty of hard, physical labor, and Nick bluffed his way into the construction business by telling the foreman he was a carpenter. The boss quickly realized that wasn't the case, but there was enough need for less-skilled labor to keep Nick gainfully employed for the better part of the year.[3]

At some point in 1907 the construction work began to peter out, and Nick got it into his head to go to Alaska for what turned out to be the tail end of the gold rush there. It didn't work out too well.

"He saw in the headlines in the newspaper that you could find gold just anywhere up there," Mary Ann recalled. "He went up there and worked a month. And all [the gold] you could get you really had to dig and dig and dig for. Some of it they could pan out of the rivers, but it was a lot of work connected with that, and it wasn't the kind of work he wanted to do. It was much too cold for him, so he came back to San Francisco."

After returning to California, Nick found that a number of his friends were talking up Watsonville, where the apple industry, largely run by Croatians, had become a thriving concern. He decided to give it a try. Ann Soldo, former mayor of Watsonville and host of a popular Croatian radio program for years, told the Pajaro Valley Historical Association in 1979 that Nick came to Watsonville with more faith and hope than worldly possessions. He rode a bicycle the 90 miles from San Francisco, Soldo said, with 50 cents in his pocket and wearing a pair of mismatching shoes — one brown and one black.

The exact date of Nick's arrival in Watsonville is unknown, but extrapolating from oral histories, it would appear to be some time in early 1908. In the 1910 census he is listed as an agricultural laborer, residing as a lodger on Walker Street. He went to work in a packing shed owned by Frank Radovan,[5] who subsequently left town following serious financial problems and resurfaced a few years later in Chile.[6] By 1912 Nick became a man of property, either leasing or purchasing, depending on the source, the Thompson Ranch near Aromas, which is still part of the family land holdings.[5]

To a modern-day reader, particularly one used to California's high land values, this may seem puzzling. How could someone who came to the area with no money and not even a decent pair of shoes be acquiring an apple orchard four years later, after doing unskilled labor in a packing shed? Some context is in order.

In the first two decades of the 20th century, the stake that was needed to buy into an apple orchard of sufficient size to be profitable was around $500. A laborer making a dollar a day, working six days a week, and saving half his earnings, could raise such a stake in three to four years. Also, life was simpler and the cost of living was significantly less in many ways. There was neither income tax, nor payroll deductions for Social Security or Medicare. It wasn't necessary to have an automobile or telephone, and radio, television, and the personal computer hadn't yet been invented. A person possessed of determination, discipline and frugality could reduce a household budget to the essentials of food, clothing and shelter, living on very little and saving the rest. Many people, Nick Borina apparently among them, did just that. It is also possible that he received a small start-up loan from fellow countrymen, as many young men in his position did.

Donna Mekis said in an interview that families in Croatia, nearly all tenant farmers, were fiercely attached to the land, and that a passion for land carried over when they emigrated to America and had a chance to become land owners.

"Absolutely the most important part of the culture was keeping land in the family," Mekis said. "Land was a really, really important thing, and to buy your own land was the number one goal of the guys who came over here. The question for them was how quick could you start buying property?"

A longtime apple grower in the Pajaro Valley, who was well acquainted with Borina and his family, offered this appraisal of Nick Borina:

"He started with nothing, but he had better knowledge and worked harder than a lot of other people. He was smart and had it in his mind to buy property and make money." The grower, who asked not to be named, added that Nick's timing was also impeccable. The apple growers who got into the business before World War I, the grower said, tended to be the ones who became most soundly established in the business.

A number of people who knew Nick in later years said he was a lifelong business innovator who often saw opportunities before others in the apple business did. One early example occurred in the fall of 1916, when Nick had been an apple grower for only four years. A shortage of railroad cars had left many growers in the Pajaro Valley sitting on stored apples they couldn't ship, but Nick took matters into his own hands. This is how Watsonville's *Evening Pajaronian* told the story in its November 11 edition:

AUTO TRUCK MAY SOLVE
SHIPPING PROBLEM

Whether or not the [railroad]* car shortage problem will be solved in the future by the transportation of apples on automobile trucks to the Bay City markets depends on the success of the trial shipment that was made today by N.M. Borina, the well known West Third Street fruit packer. This morning he loaded 410 boxes of apples on Bart Driscoll's auto truck and trailer and with Driscoll at the wheel, the load started for Oakland.

Mr. Borina was forced to ship his apples to Oakland by truck or lose a profitable sale. There were no "reefers" [refrigerated cars]* in the local railroad yards and the chances were slim of getting any within the next few days so Borina decided upon an experiment that may yet threaten to revolutionize the shipment of apples to state points not too far distant from Watsonville.

Mr. Borina states that two trips in three days can be made to the San Francisco Bay section by the present service. The shipping of apples from the valley by auto trucks has long been discussed by fruit men of the community but Borina is the first man to start a trial trip. The fruit men of the city are watching for the results of Borina's experiment, and if it is a success the car shortage problem may in future years be far from a serious trouble. The automobile truck may yet revolutionize the transportation of apples in the state of California.

Given the state of roads and the reliability of motor vehicles at the time, it was quite a gamble, and for whatever reason, the newspaper never followed up on the story, so the fate of that first shipment is lost to history. But the last sentence of the news story turned out to be true, and whether or not Nick's initial venture in that regard was a success, he was the first to try an innovation, shipping by truck, that became a lasting and fundamental part of the apple business within the next two decades.

*Bracketed text indicates corrections or additions made to the original by the editor of this book.

He also was becoming, early in his career, a prosperous young man, a fact that can be ascertained by reading between the lines of several news stories. When World War I broke out in 1917, Nick sought exemption from the draft on the grounds that he was still a citizen of the Austro-Hungarian Empire (he didn't become a U.S. citizen until 1926), but he was a generous contributor to the Liberty Loan Fund, which raised bond money to support the war effort. In a little over a year, he contributed at least $800, according to newspaper reports — an amount greater than the average workingman's annual salary at the time. In 1918, when the recently enacted federal income tax was still a novelty, the names of those who paid it were put up in the Post Office for all to see. Nick Borina was on the list.

A single young man in possession of a growing fortune typically begins to think of marrying and starting a family. Young Nick Borina would have been quite a catch, and in keeping with the culture of the time, he would have been looking for a mate in Watsonville's close-knit Croatian community, where everybody knew everybody else, and where family connections often led to matchmaking. When, where, and how they met is unknown, but because newspapers of that time were eager to print the names of local residents for any reason, we do know that by the summer of 1916, Nick already had been introduced to the widow who would become his wife, Lucy, ten months later. The knowledge comes from a personal item in the Watsonville *Evening Pajaronian* of July 31, 1916, which read in full:

> Joseph Secondo, Mr. and Mrs. L. Secondo, Mrs. [Lucy] Bakich, Mrs. Jerenich [Jerinich] and Mr. Borino [Borina] of this city attended the Austrian military picnic at Oakland yesterday.

Lucy Secondo. Everybody described her as "tough"; not surprising considering that she had to cope with the murder of her first husband less than a month into the marriage. Ten years after that, at the age of 29, she married Nick Borina.

———◦◦◦———

Chapter 2

Lucy Secondo

Like Nick Borina, Lucy Secondo came from the Dalmatian coast to the United States at a young age. She was 13 when she arrived in New York in 1901 on the *S.S. Statendam*, sailing from Rotterdam, Holland. Unlike her future husband, she followed her father, who had come here nearly a decade earlier and eventually reunited with his family in a more prosperous new world.

Lucy was born February 27, 1888, in Lovorno, south of Dubrovnik, to Mato Sekondo (the spelling of the last name was changed in the U.S.) and his wife, the former Marija Radin. Mato, who was known as Martin in America, was a descendant of the Kapetanić family. In the mid 1800s, one branch of the Sekondo family in Lovorno had no sons, and Martin's father, Josip Kapetanić, married a daughter of this family, taking her last name, as was a custom at the time.

Martin was born in Lovorno March 17, 1851, and grew up, married and started a family, which eventually included six sons: Joseph, John (who died in his youth), Martin, Louis, Mitchell, and Peter; and two daughters, Kate and Lucy. In 1892 he left the Dalmatian coast to seek his fortune in America.

In an oral history interview conducted by UC-Santa Cruz, Martin's granddaughter Mary Ann Radovich recalled how the story of Martin's emigration had been passed down through the family in gen-

Martin Secondo (1851-1930), father of Lucy Secondo Borina, first arrived in Watsonville in 1892.

Lucy Secondo (left) and her parents, Martin and Mary Radin Secondo. Photo taken around 1901, the year Lucy and her mother arrived in Watsonville.

eral terms. Noting that people from the Dalmatian coast had been flocking to America for years, she continued:

"Letters would come back, telling people about life here [in America]. They would compare notes, naturally. When things were good over there [Dalmatia], when there was no crop failure, no bad winters, no other problems, people would not think about [emigrating]. There was no way for those people to build up enough money as a reserve to live on. It was just a hand-to-mouth business. You grew food this year for winter and maybe next spring … they were all serfs … So anyway, I guess my grandfather probably was building up all this information about what was happening over here, and then when either the first crop failed or something, he felt that he knew enough about what was going on over here to know that maybe that [coming to America] was the best thing to do."

After traveling by sea to New York and taking the train to California, Martin wound up in the town of Jackson, in the Gold Country, where many men of Slav descent had congregated because of readily available mining jobs. According to Radovich, he didn't care for the work in the mines and kept looking, finally deciding, after a couple of years, to come to Watsonville to work in the thriving, largely Croatian-run apple business there.

In Watsonville, Martin Secondo followed a path that Nick Borina and other immigrants would later take. He began as a laborer and saved everything he could. He eventually was able to rent his own apple orchard from the prominent Wyckoff family and later brought a couple of his sons over from Dalmatia. From the beginning as apple farmers, he and his sons expanded into the apple packing business and prospered in it as well. His oldest son, Joseph, followed him in 1893;

The Secondo family. After the murder of her first husband, Lucy Secondo Bakich moved in with her brother Joe, who oversaw her financial affairs. Joe is standing in above left photo, with his sisters, Lucy (right) and Kate. Above right: Joe (standing) with brothers Martin (left) and possibly John, circa 1899. Lower left is Lucy and her brother, Peter, shortly after they arrived in 1901. Lower right shows Louis Secondo (standing) with brothers Mitchell (left) and Joe.

the next two oldest sons, John and Martin came over in 1899 (John died that same year); then the remaining three sons, Louis, Mitchell, and Peter, the two daughters, Kate and Lucy, and his wife came over in 1901.

Not much is known about Lucy's early years in Watsonville. Radovich, her daughter, said she received a basic education but not much more:

"She went to school, I believe, for about a year. It was less than a year. To the Sisters' school, but it just wasn't the thing to do for them because they were poor. They had to work and my mother said that it was decided as long as she could read and write that was adequate. So they went to work."

The few surviving photos of young Lucy show an attractive woman with a keen, penetrating gaze. Unlike most people of her day, she could look at a camera without flinching or freezing. People who knew her later in life invariably describe her as "tough," an impression she might understandably have projected, given some of the turns her life took.

By the time she was in her late teens, Lucy had a number of men interested in her. "Several men wanted to marry my sister," her brother Louis later said, "but when Bakich came along she decided that she liked him better than any of the others." That would be Luke Bakich, 32 years old, a resident of Watsonville for six years (about as long as Lucy), and a member of the Bakich & Scurich apple-packing business. Bakich had been born in the village of Čilipi, about seven miles from where Lucy was born. The *Evening Pajaronian* reported their impending union in its edition of March 30, 1907:

The wedding of Miss Lucy Secondo, daughter of Mr. and Mrs. Secondo, and Luke Bakich, a prominent fruit packer of this city, is announced to take place tomorrow, Easter Sunday. After the ceremony the young couple will leave for San Francisco, and on their return will take up their residence in Watsonville. Many congratulations will attend their marriage.

Shortly after her 19th birthday, Lucy had married the man she chose from among several suitors — a man with excellent prospects who had built his bride a new house at 509 Rodriguez Street,[7] in the heart of what later became Watsonville's Slav district. Everything appeared to be in place for a happy and prosperous future; then, less than a month after the wedding, it changed in an instant.

On the morning of Saturday, April 27, Luke Bakich left his home on Rodriguez Street at daybreak, planning to ride his bicycle to oversee spraying operations at a new orchard his firm had secured in the Amesti district, a few miles outside the city limits of Watsonville at that time. Shortly before 6 a.m., a local painter, L. Ritter, saw Bakich pushing his bicycle up the Santa Cruz Road (now Freedom Boulevard). It was the last time he was seen alive.

About 20 minutes later, a Freedom blacksmith, D.F. Fulmer, was on his way to work when a laborer riding with him saw a man lying by the side of the road near some bushes and weeds. It was Bakich, already dead from repeated blows to the head with a redwood picket ripped from a nearby fence and possibly a metal pipe as well. That night's *Evening Pajaronian* described it as "the most vindictive as well as brutal occurrence which has ever taken place in this peaceful valley."

The crime was a local sensation and attracted media coverage as far away as San Francisco. Sheriff Howard Trafton, who personally oversaw the investigation said that it was not likely to have been a robbery, but was probably a case of revenge. Initial speculation centered on the idea that the killer might be a former suitor of Lucy's who had lost out to Bakich, but that line of inquiry never panned out. The funeral for Bakich was held two days later and was reported in the *Evening Pajaronian*:

> The funeral of the late Luke Bakich, who was so cruelly murdered last Saturday afternoon by some unknown scoundrel, took place this morning from the home he had so recently built and furnished on upper Rodriguez Street. A requiem high mass was celebrated at St. Patrick's church, and the large edifice was crowded with friends of the deceased who had come to pay their respects to the memory of one who had never been known to harbor an ill will against any person. The pallbearers were F.P. Marinovich, Luke Scurich, Mateo Lettunich, Antone Scurich, Peter Stolich and John Scurich.

The pallbearers, as historian Donna Mekis noted, "were the heaviest hitters in town," a sign that the Croatian community rallied around the murder victim. Local Slavs also raised $675, offered as a reward for information leading to the capture of the killer, with the sheriff adding another $50 to the pot. It did no good. Within a week, all lines of investigation had run cold, and the case remains unsolved more than a century later.

And so, a month after her marriage, Lucy Bakich was alone again. "There was a lot of baggage to being a widow in that community," Mekis said. A woman would be expected to observe a long period of mourning, wearing black the entire time, and would typically move into her father's home. But Lucy's father, Martin, was by then living apart from his wife, Marija, a situation that continued until Marija's death in 1917, so Lucy joined her mother in the home of her oldest brother, Joseph.

Joseph Secondo was appointed special administrator of Bakich's estate, which was valued at $5,750 (approximately $300,000 in today's money). Bakich had died intestate, and Lucy was his only heir. Over the next ten years, Lucy appeared in the newspapers from time to time in connection with the sorts of public-record financial transactions that were commonly reported in those days. The pattern appeared to be that her brother gradually deeded property to her as she grew older and was better able to manage it, and that she worked for the family's packing business as well. According to her daughter Mary Ann, she worked at Nick Borina's packing house, but it was not clear from the context of the interview whether she had known him before working for him.

Socially, she became involved with the Companions of the Forest, a group that might have been known, in the language of the time, as the ladies' auxiliary of the International Order of Foresters. The Foresters were a fraternal organization, similar to the Moose and Elks, and also offered insurance policies and benefits. In April of 1910 she was reported to be in attendance at a reception sponsored by the group, and in July 1911 was installed as Left Guide of the Pajaro Valley Rose Circle, Companions of the Forest. At a January 1912 ceremony, the Foresters and Companions held a joint installation of officers and Lucy was sworn in as Left Guard. A senior officer of the Foresters at the same time was M. Secondo, almost certainly her brother Mitchell.

Under the customs of the Slav community at the time, Lucy, as a childless widow, would have been free to remarry after the mourning period. (A widow with children had fewer options.) Living with her mother and brother, Mekis said, "She would have had a lot of support, but it wouldn't have been easy … there would have been a lot of gossip about the murder, but you get the sense that Lucy was a beautiful, proud woman who would hold her head high."

Lucy lived as a widow for a little over ten years before marrying Nick Borina. That was not an exceptionally long gap between marriages at the time, but it raises the question, which can never be answered definitively, of how the circumstances of her life affected her view of what a woman should expect. Mekis wonders if having a father who lived apart from his wife contributed to a belief in a woman's need for self-reliance, and about the effect of Luke Bakich's murder. "If the mother (Lucy) had the traumatic experience of getting married early and losing her husband, it's not likely she would have pressed her daughters to get married early."

In any event, Lucy remarried after ten years, in May 1917. She was 29 on the wedding day, and Nick Borina was 27.

The Borina Wedding. Group photo (above) taken after the ceremony, most likely, from the design of the building, at the Borina packing house. Closer shot, below, of the bride and groom, flanking young Martin Secondo, son of Lucy's brother, Mitchell. Older woman with glasses behind the couple is Lucy's mother, Marija Radin Secondo.

Chapter 3

The Borina Family

Nick Borina and Lucy (Secondo) Bakich were married May 13, 1917, and judging from the handful of photographs that survive, it was a fairly large and well attended event. The *Evening Pajaronian* two days later carried this report:

> Nick Borina, one of the leading fruit packers of this city, and Mrs. Lucy Bakich, also of this city, were married last Sunday at noon in St. Patrick's Church. Mrs. L. Arbanas, a sister of the bride, was the bridesmaid, and the groom was attended by his brother, M. Borina [Martin] of San Francisco. After the ceremony the guests adjourned to the home of the bride, where a sumptuous wedding feast was enjoyed, which was followed by music, dancing, and other forms of entertainment.
>
> Mrs. Borina is the daughter of Mr. and Mrs. M. Secondo of this city and is well known here as a charming young woman. The groom has been engaged in the apple shipping business here for several years and is an estimable young man.

Within three years of the wedding, two daughters arrived, completing the family. Mary Ann, the first, was born October 16, 1918. Her sister, June Doris, followed shortly, on January 4, 1920. Over the next couple of decades the Borinas were a close, tightly knit family group. They were all deeply involved in the family business, and the daughters grew up learning the ins and outs of apple growing and

Starting a life together. Nick and Lucy on their wedding day. They complemented each other well, bringing different attributes to their marriage and the family business.

packing. They were also raised to take care of themselves if need be and were supported in pursuing a level of education that few of their peers, male or female, would attain.

Those years also saw the growth of the Borina apple business into one of the largest of the Pajaro Valley. Some say Borina was the biggest apple grower/shipper in the region, a claim that can't be proved since most such concerns were privately held. But he clearly was at the top tier of the field, growing and prospering as the Santa Cruz County apple industry reached its peak in the 1920s, then continuing to thrive even as apples began a gradual but steady decline over the next two decades. The success of the business in Nick's lifetime and beyond was a family effort.

■

AFTER THE BIRTH of Mary Ann and June, Lucy Borina went to work in the family business nearly every day. A few years after Nick and Lucy's marriage, Nick's brother Martin moved down from San Francisco, married Stella Šapro, who had arrived in Watsonville from the old country in 1921, and settled in working for Nick in the business and living on one of the ranches on San Juan Road in north Monterey County. Nick and his family lived at 57 Brennan Street in Watsonville, which was renumbered 103 Brennan by the Post Office in 1925.

(Two of Nick's sisters from the old country also moved to America and settled in the Watsonville area, but were not involved in the family business. Mary (1897-1991) married John Violich in Watsonville in a double wedding ceremony in 1922, along with Martin and his wife. They had no children. Nike "Nicolina" (1900-1974) married Peter Rajkovich in 1923; their family lived in San Jose and Hollister.)

Mother and daughters. From the beginning, June and Mary Ann were raised to be self-sufficient and to value education. Left, June (in mother's lap) and Mary Ann with Lucy, Aug. 15, 1920; right, 1926 photo with June on left.

Proud Papa. Nick Borina with daughters (June at left) on Christmas Day, 1925. Mary Ann has been described as being like the son Nick never had, and when June was named District Attorney, he put her letter of appointment on the wall at his office.

Nick continued to acquire property during that time. Reports in the *Evening Pajaronian* had him purchasing the MacDonald Packing House on West Third Street[8] and buying, with his sometime business partner James J. Crowley, 134 acres of the original Redman Ranch. What was reported in the newspapers was only the tip of the iceberg, as Nick tended not to seek publicity. The Borina family over the years acquired numerous commercial properties in the cities of Watsonville and Salinas, diversifying its holdings rather than sticking strictly to agriculture.

Years later, Mary Ann would tell her neighbor, John Ivanovich, about the family dynamic, in which Nick was the speculator but Lucy acted as a restraining influence.

"She [Mary Ann] admired her father," Ivanovich said. "She said he was the one who was willing to take risks and buy another piece of property. If her mother had allowed it, he [Nick] probably would have owned half the property in California."

In farming, Nick was willing to try new ideas. Apple growers in those days often planted row crops, usually beans or beets, to make use

On the job. Nick Borina spraying at the Riverside Road ranch; he often jumped in and did a job himself if no one else was available.

of the land left open in the spacing between young apple trees, which were planted 24 to 30 feet apart. Nick was the first, or one of the first, to plant raspberries between the trees, and generated more income from them than he would have from vegetables. In March of 1923 the recently formed Berry Growers Assn. of the Pajaro Valley named Nick chair of the raspberry committee. A year later he was one of 15 directors named to the board of the newly incorporated Watsonville Apple Distributors, one of several organizations formed over the years in an attempt to get local apple growers to work together in shipping and selling their crops.

One other aspect of Nick's farming skills is worth mentioning in passing. He had a gift for dowsing, or using a divining rod to find water beneath the surface of the ground, and was sometimes consulted by other farmers who wanted his advice as to where to drill a well. One old-timer, who was a young boy at the time, recalls Nick being brought over to the family farm to advise in such a case. Nearly seven decades later, he still remembers, as any boy would, how awed he was when Nick let him hold the dowsing rod.[9]

The handful of people who still remember Nick and Lucy Borina from those days say that they were tirelessly committed to the business and often raised their voices at their employees and at each other — not necessarily in a mean way, but shouting was part of their communication style.

Millie Davis, the daughter of Lucy's brother Louis Secondo, used to play with the Borina daughters at their ranch and packing shed. Nick, she said, worked mostly in the shed, so she didn't see him much, but had a strong recollection that, "He was shrewd, a goer. He didn't give up." When she married her husband, George Davis, in the

1940s, George was thinking of becoming a farmer, so she introduced him to Nick Borina and urged him to have a long conversation with Nick about what the business would entail, because she wanted him to hear it from the best source. George eventually decided against farming and went on to become a highly successful general contractor.

John Radin, former Watsonville City Manager, also knew the Borinas as a boy in the 1930s and '40s. Of Nick, he said, "He was a tough old guy. I was more scared of him than anything. He yelled and screamed at the people in the packing shed." He also recalled Nick and Lucy shouting at each other, but in a way that seemed to be their affectionate style of communication. "How those two got together, I don't know," Radin said. "They yelled and screamed at each other, but I guess they were two peas in a pod."

A letter from Mary Ann to June when June was at Stanford years later recalls an incident of Nick's bluster that indicates it was part of his business intensity and was taken with a grain of salt by those who knew him. The letter was dated Sept. 27, 1939, and describes what happened when a man nicknamed "Grapes" came to pick up a large load of apples from the packing shed and forgot to remove an iron chained to the truck:

Well, Grapes comes in to sign the tags, which I wrote out for him, then goes out the front door, hops into the truck, starts 'er off, and then crash, zam ... rrrrrkkkk. The trailer pulled the iron along and bent the corner post and the corrugated iron so that it looked almost like a dog's hind leg. I was by the grader and turned around as soon as I heard the crash. I noticed the iron and then yelled at him to stop. Pa jumps out of the office, stringing out a line of G.D. S.O.B's, "bunch of boneheads," bla, bla,

bla. Then he and Frank get busy and yank the thing in place again. It
looks alright now, although with slightly a patched-up look.

An unusual aspect of the Borina operations was that Nick primarily worked in the packing house, while Lucy mostly supervised the
men in the fields, an uncommon occupation for a woman at the time,
even one universally described as "tough." When Mary Ann took over
day-to-day operations of the business years later, she worked from the
packing house, and later her home, while her husband dealt with the
field workers. In the oral history interview, she recalled her mother's
contribution:

"Well, my mother, she watched a lot of the field operations. She
also helped in the packing house. She also watched for different pest
problems and growth problems. You have to watch your orchards,
watch the conditions. If a tree looks yellow at the wrong time of the
year you know there's something wrong with it. It's something that
has to be watched daily, and she was involved in that."

Millie Davis described Lucy as, "a pleasant person. She was very
interested in her work — she liked to make a buck." But at the same
time she has vivid memories of Lucy riding herd over the field hands
in the orchards, while the girls played nearby. "She'd just holler at the
help, and we could hear it because she had a pretty loud voice." Radin
had a similar recollection of Lucy's relations with employees. "She was
assertive. I'd compare her to some of the first sergeants I knew in the
Army. She was probably a hard person to work for."

A couple of anecdotes were told by several different people about
Lucy in the orchards; they may have been apocryphal, but the fact
they were still remembered after all these years suggests that people felt

they were in some way true to her character. One story was that she carried a pistol (in some accounts it was pearl-handled) in her purse for protection while out in the fields. (In June Borina's family photo albums, there are a couple of photos of Lucy with hunting rifles and birds she had shot, so she was clearly no stranger to firearms.)

Another story had Lucy in the orchards, probably during pruning season, when one of the field hands came down the ladder from his tree and began walking toward another row of trees. Lucy shouted at him, demanding to know where he was going. He explained that he had to urinate. "Do it here by the ladder," she reportedly said. "I don't want you walking around while I'm paying you by the hour."

In today's highly regulated workplaces, a story like that can be hard to fathom, but it needs to be placed in a historical context. Many Slav families in the Pajaro Valley laughingly tell similar stories about the flintiness of their ancestors. The first generation of immigrants knew what it was to have nothing, worked unbelievably hard to become successful, kept a close eye on money, and respected others who themselves worked hard. Indeed, Donna Mekis said, "The best thing you could say about somebody in that community was, 'He's a good worker.'"

By the mid-1920s, Nick had been in the country a quarter of a century and was well assimilated. He continued to send money back home to his mother, but never returned to the Old Country again. On December 9, 1924, he petitioned for citizenship, with rancher James J. Crowley and insurance agent Eugene McSherry as his witnesses. On May 6, 1925, the petition was denied without prejudice owing to an unspecified problem with McSherry's testimony. A little more than a year later Nick reapplied, with Frank J. Scrivani replacing McSherry as

Handy with a gun. Lucy Secondo Bakich (left) and her sister Kate Arbanas on a bird-hunting outing, location and date unknown but probably before the marriage to Nick Borina. Lucy was later rumored to carry a pistol in her purse when she worked in the Borina orchards.

A Watsonville childhood. Mary Ann and June had a typical childhood in many respects. Above right: Mary Ann's sixth birthday party, October 1924; from left: Bobby Capitanich, June, Mary Ann, Margaret Capitanich and Anna Scurich. Left: Mary Ann in her new birthday dress, October 1927.

Childhood friends. Anita (left) and Mildred Secondo were frequent play-mates of the Borina girls, and as daughters of Lucy's brother Louis, first cousins as well. Millie went on to marry contractor George Davis, and at the age of 95 still had vivid memories of playing with the Borina girls.

the second witness, and on December 8, 1926, he was admitted as a U.S. citizen. In the 1930 census, Lucy was also shown as being a U.S. citizen; by that time the Borinas had become an American family.

■

MARY ANN AND JUNE had a childhood that was in some ways typical for a reasonably prosperous family of the time, but in other ways not typical at all. Mary Ann was stricken with polio at an early age, and for the rest of her life was limited in her mobility, though able to walk. Millie Davis, who was almost two years older than Mary Ann, spent a lot of time with the Borina girls in the 1920s. Her mother, the former Marie Jerinich, would make dresses every year for Millie, her sister Anita, and the Borina sisters, and often drove them to the Borina ranch on Riverside Road to play.

There was a windmill on the property that helped draw water from a well, and they played near it, she recalls. Games included jump rope (Mary Ann usually held the rope; her polio kept her from jumping much), jacks, tag, hopscotch, and going out into the orchard and climbing trees. In an *Evening Pajaronian* social article on October 17, 1924, Millie and Anita (along with their mother) were listed as being among the 15 guests at Mary Ann's sixth birthday party.

What was particularly unusual about Mary Ann and June's upbringing was that they seem to have been encouraged, more than most young women of their generation, to be ready to take care of themselves later on. In the UCSC oral history interview, Mary Ann got into that issue when interviewer Meri Knaster asked how the Great Depression had particularly affected her:

Mary Ann: Well, I guess that's one of the reasons that I went to work, because my parents weren't sure what the future held. When there is a depression, and nobody knows the length of it or the severity of it, they wanted to prepare my sister and me for living. They felt that if they gave us a life of leisure and that wasn't what was to be, it would not have been the proper training to get.

Knaster: That's interesting that they considered you might have to take care of yourself.

Mary Ann: Sure.

Knaster: They didn't just expect you to get married or that the natural course for any woman was to be taken care of by a man.

Mary Ann: Well, not really. My mother and father didn't really think that way.

Knaster: That's fairly progressive! (laughter)

Mary Ann: Yes, they both were. My mother in particular. She was very progressive and thought that women should not be clinging vines. She thought that if they were going to get married, they should help their husbands. And if they were not going to get married, help themselves.

Knaster: That is very progressive. And two good examples came out of that philosophy.

Both Mary Ann and June excelled in school, and their parents clearly encouraged and supported their efforts, sending them to private school and later to Stanford. Mary Ann doesn't mention parental pressure in her oral interview, and Millie Davis said, "They were all serious about school, but their mother never pushed them. They just had a mind of their own … they were very, very devoted to church, to school …"

At the beginning of the 1924 school year, Mary Ann, a few weeks less than six years old, began school at Moreland Notre Dame, a Catholic school just down the street from the Borina home. June, a bit more than four and a half at the time, was upset at her sister's departure and wanted to go to school herself. She apparently made such a fuss over it that her parents and the Sisters at the school relented and admitted her. Christine Grul, the current principal at the school, said that the story has been passed down over the years about how young June spent much of her first year in Sister Veronica's lap, but that after that the two sisters went through school together as equals, both graduating in 1936.

Their education at Moreland Notre Dame covered not only the fundamentals of the day, but also a great emphasis on language and music. They studied Latin, French and Spanish, which along with their native Croatian and English, made them proficient in five languages. June and Mary Ann also showed a talent for music, both becoming accomplished on more than one instrument. June played violin and piano, and as an adult had a piano in her home and would often play it. Across the board, they excelled academically. Fran Dobler, a niece of Martin Borina through his wife's side, went to Moreland Notre Dame years after June and Mary Ann and recalls one of the nuns telling her at the time, "Those Borina women were smart."

Their educational attainment was uncommon, to say the least, for the time. In an era when most men didn't go to college and few women did, Mary Ann and June both went to Stanford after high school and graduated in 1940. Tom Ninkovich, a historian of Watsonville's Slav community, says that as far as his research indicates, June and Mary Ann were the first second-generation female Croatians to attend Stanford.

School days. Though 15 months apart in age, Mary Ann and June went to school together and were in the same class. Above, sophomore class photo from Moreland Notre Dame Academy, 1933; June is third from left in back row, Mary Ann far right back row. Below, left, 7th grade softball team, 1931, with June at lower right. Bottom right, June in the school orchestra, middle row, left. Both daughters were accomplished with musical instruments.

The experience of getting a first-class education clearly meant a lot to both June and Mary Ann and was something they valued throughout their lives. In the UCSC oral history interview, Mary Ann said of her childhood, "I can't say that we were denied anything that we really needed. Because in those days having a college education was more than what the average person got." June's goddaughter, Sheila Burke, recalls that June was always telling her about the importance of a good education and how the chance to get a college education was a gift that shouldn't be squandered. "To her, education was everything," Burke said. With that attitude, it should not have been surprising that June went on to get a law degree from Stanford in 1942, when she was only 22.

Another aspect of the family life was that the Borinas traveled a great deal. A scrapbook of June's that still survives contains numerous photographs taken all around California and in Washington State, where Lucy's brother Martin had moved. Burke said that in later years June recalled trips to Honolulu in the 1930s in connection with her father's Asian ventures (discussed in more detail in the next section). And as they got old enough to drive and went to college, the daughters had automobiles. Historian Mekis said that travel was important to the Slavs who came to America, and it appeared to be something, in addition to education, that was a significant part of the Borina family experience. Both June and Mary Ann traveled considerably as adults, in June's case often as part of her husband's far-flung judicial assignments.

That's not to say the family was always free and easy with a dollar. In the oral history interview, Mary Ann recalled with vivid specificity a time she was denied something she wanted.

Law school days. June's photo album has many shots from her Stanford Law School period. Taking a break from studying with a popular magazine (upper right), making music with the Bairos sisters (left and upper left), and two friends, Charlotte and Jeannie, with June's Cadillac coupe, Daisy Belle, in front of her home at 488 Harvard St., Palo Alto. There are no photos of June from her graduation, but she took several of her classmates that day (below).

Well traveled. The Borina family traveled extensively in the Western U.S., Mexico, and Hawaii as the daughters were growing up. Travel photos from June's scrapbooks.

◄June and her mother, Lucy, summer of 1938 at Donner Pass.

June (right) and Mary Ann, San Pedro, Calif., 1935.►

◄June (right) and friends at Sawmill Flats, Washington, in June 1940.

June (left) and Mary Ann, Agua Caliente, Mexico, July 4, 1935.►

Mary Ann: … A lot of frivolities of life … I missed at the time. There were fashions of men, just like there are now. And there were … things I couldn't get because my mother just thought they were unnecessary. I remember one handbag that I wanted so badly. Because at that time when I was in high school, some of the girls had them. They were little dogs with the zipper on top. And you carried your little dog to school with you. They were made to look like real dogs, you know. They were about that big.

Knaster: That looks like a foot long.

Mary Ann: Yes. About like so. And with the zipper on top was the part where the handbag was. I wanted one so badly. I knew exactly what I wanted, because this girlfriend of mine had one. It was grey, and it was just the cutest little thing. And I came home to my mother, I remember this very clearly, and I explained it to her. I gave her the complete description, and the size, and all that, and without batting an eye, she says, "No." I told her, "Well, how come I can't have it?" And she said, "Just because you don't need it." And that was it. The way she said I didn't need it stopped that right there. (laughter)

■

THE GREAT DEPRESSION took its toll on the apple industry, as it did on nearly every other. There were no crop reports done for Santa Cruz County at the time (those came along after World War II, as the county Agricultural Commissioner's office grew in size and influence), but the U.S. Department of Agriculture maintained some statistics that gave an indication of the effect.

In its 1929 Agricultural Census, conducted in the last year of the

Roaring Twenties, the USDA placed the value of the California apple crop at $8,065,046, based on statewide sales of 145,741 tons of apples. Five years later, in 1934, at close to the depth of the Depression, the total value of the state apple crop had dropped in the USDA Census to $4,791,078, even as the tonnage (145,537) barely changed. As much as anything else, that reflected the sharp drop in all values caused by Depression deflation. (To get a rough idea of the value of the money in 2013 dollars, the 1934 figure should be multiplied by a factor of at least 30.)

Santa Cruz County in 1934 accounted for 40 percent of both the state's apple tonnage (58,965) and sales revenue ($1,916,431.12). From July of 1934 to June of 1935, a period reflecting sales of the 1934 apple crop, Nick Borina's revenues, determined from a company ledger on file at the Agricultural History Project near Watsonville, were in excess of $200,000. The sales reflected his own apples as well as those he sold for other growers, and some of the revenue may have represented berries, pears, and other non-apple sales, but it would nonetheless appear that close to 10 percent of Santa Cruz County's apples, and maybe more, went through Nick Borina's packing shed before reaching their final destination.

And an impressive packing operation it was. A trade newspaper called the *National Agricultural News*, which was printed in California, ran a front-page story in August of 1935, under the headline: "Borina Apple Plant Is the Last Word in Apple Packing." Calling the Borina facility "one of the finest combinations of apple packing and storage units in the state of California," the article read in part:

> First a grower, then in turn adding a packing establishment to his business, [Borina] has developed into one of the most successful packers and

The Borina Brand. Fruit labels from the Borinas' operations over the years. Bottom label reflects the daughters adding "M.A. and J. Borina" over their father's name on the label after his death in 1949.

Pacific Theme. Some of Borina's apples bound for Asia went out under the Diamond Head label, probably a gesture toward Wing Coffee Co. of Honolulu, which distributed the fruit.

Banding Together. Borina also distributed apples under the label of the Watsonville Apple Growers and Packers Association, a group with which he had a falling-out in the late 1930s.

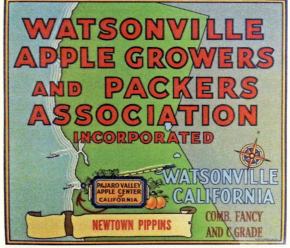

shippers in the state ... last year handling more than 350,000 boxes of apples and shipping 400 [rail] cars from the Watsonville district. Of these he grows approximately 250,000 boxes of apples on 250 acres of fine orchard land, in addition to shipping 20 cars of pears.

His apple yield consists of Newtown Pippins, Pearmains and Bellflowers, with some peaches. Besides he grows 40 to 50 acres of lettuce during a fiscal year, but does not pack the lettuce.

In his packing and storage plant, which is 238 feet square [238 x 238 feet], covering 1½ acres, with two late models of combination graders and two washing machines (Cutler) he has a packing capacity of 5,000 boxes a day and employs 40 people the year round, with a daily working force during the busy season of 100 persons.

His storage plant, under the same roof with his packing plant, but in a separate department, has a storing capacity of 100,000 square feet, which enables him to produce, pack and sell with profitable results. He is ably assisted by his wife and daughters, both students of the highest accredited qualifications in the Watsonville High School. *[Actually, they were at Moreland Notre Dame.]*

So in the midst of the Great Depression, the Borina apple business seemed to be thriving. Another paragraph in the same story provides much of the explanation.

His [Borina's] Clover Brand and N.M.B. Best, 90 percent of which are shipped to foreign lands, have made his products international in scope ... and has added prestige to Watsonville apples in these countries, many of them going to Honolulu, China, the Philippines and other far lands.

Apples from the Watsonville area had been going to Europe for some time, and to Asia in small numbers, but by the late 1920s, California fruit growers were beginning to look to the Asian market as a possible way of raising sales and revenues. Following the end of World War I, there was a shakeout in California agriculture. Simply put, land in the Golden State was more expensive than that in the Midwest, making it next to impossible for California grain growers to compete. Many converted to fruit crops in response, but by the end of the 1920s, domestic fruit consumption had stabilized, with little domestic growth potential in a depressed economy.

Asia, with its population of nearly a billion people, was an inviting (but difficult) market. On April 26, 1928, the *Evening Pajaronian* reported that the Watsonville Kiwanis Club heard a talk from Frank Ryan of the John Demartini Company, San Francisco fruit and produce brokers, about the potential market for local apples in Asia. He optimistically painted a picture of a huge market, but one that would be challenging to crack. The biggest problems, he said, were the lack of cold storage facilities in Asia, difficulties of transporting perishable goods long distances, dealing with large numbers of small retail merchants, and finding a way to sell to a huge but poor consumer base that would be buying apples as luxury items, one at a time.

An article titled "Fruit Markets in Eastern Asia," by B.H. Crocheron and W.J. Norton, which appeared in the April 1930 issue of the *California Agricultural Experiment Station Bulletin*, and was funded through a grant from the Giannini Foundation for Agricultural Economics, echoed those concerns and added a few more. One was the question of finding a reliable Asian representative to move the product. The article noted that many agents and companies representing American and European businesses in Asia handled so many different products for so many different companies that they couldn't always do justice to all their clients. Plus, there were certain occupational hazards to doing business in the tropics. "It is common throughout the entire Far East for Europeans to work five hours or less a day," Crocheron and Norton wrote. "Often these hours are rendered ineffective by other hours that come between."

Nevertheless, the Asian market remained a tantalizing possibility. That paper reported that in 1930, only 0.2 percent of U.S. apples grown were exported to Asia. The question, Crocheron and Norton wrote, "is not the buying power of the population, but whether those who have the buying power can be induced to include California fruits among the luxuries they purchase. Would this repay the time, energy and money expended" to try to reach that market?

The immense Asian market clearly wasn't, in a figure of speaking, low-hanging fruit just waiting for someone to come along and pluck it. Yet somehow, Nick Borina was able to rise to the challenge and create a thriving Asian market for Watsonville apples — his own and others — and do it on his own without the aid of an industry association.

That Nick succeeded in Asia is well known among Watsonville-area apple people, as is the fact that he was able to take a less-common type of apple, the White Winter Pearmain, and turn it into a hot commodity along the Pacific Rim. Longtime apple grower Ray Travers recalled in a 1977 UC-Santa Cruz oral history interview:

"At one time in this valley when I was a child [Travers was born in 1921] they used to export a lot of apples into China and the Far East, and they liked their apples. They liked the Pearmain apple that used to be raised here. It was a very small apple and we used to pick it very green, but it had a big market in China. A lot of those apples were packed, and there are still a few of those trees around, but they're generally used for processing fruit nowadays."

In another oral history interview, conducted in April 1987 by

Zalia Kennedy under the sponsorship of the Pajaro Valley Historical Association and the American Association of University Women History Project, apple growers Pete Stolich and Steve Zupan had the following exchange:

Zupan: So dad decided to pull them [diseased pear trees] out and planted a new orchard in 1930. They were White Winter Pearmains, because that was a hot apple in them days to ship to China and Japan. You picked that crop before the Newtowns came in. You picked that generally about … I think it was in July somewhere. Came in early. Dad figured there was enough money there almost to pay for the harvesting of the Newtown crop when it came, trying to balance out the cost of the intake and outtake of monies coming in and out.

Stolich: I told her [interviewer Kennedy] all about Nick Borina.

Zupan: Well, yes. He was a big shipper. My dad sold apples to him. The Pearmains. He was the one who actually started the export on White Winter Pearmains. He was the kingpin on that. He really helped this valley quite a bit. A hundred percent, really! He really got it going and he was a big shipper on that. He was the strength.

Yet while everyone in the business knows that Nick established a lucrative Asian market for Watsonville apples, the details of how he did it remain shrouded in mystery. It's always possible that something will turn up at a future date, but it appears that no one in the Borina family thought to set the story down for posterity. The company ledger that survives and is held at the Agricultural History Project suggests a few clues, but because of the bare-bones nature of its entries offers no definitive answers.

One thing the ledger makes clear is that the Borina apple business had a long-standing relationship with the Wing Coffee Company, which had offices in Honolulu and Hong Kong and sold fresh fruit and fruit products in addition to coffee. Given the difficulties involved in finding a reliable agent or representative for the Asian market, it would have made sense to connect with an established business (Wing was founded in 1904) that was already handling fruit throughout Asia. The tantalizing and still unanswered question is how and where the connection was made between Borina and Wing Coffee Company. Company founder C.S. Wing visited the United States in 1925 and established a mainland branch office on Montgomery Street in San Francisco, primarily for the purpose of marketing Kona coffee in the United States. Perhaps that was where Borina and Wing connected, but no evidence exists one way or the other. Wing Coffee Company still exists as a small, Honolulu-based company, but current president Peter Kam said in an email that much to his regret, most of the company's history (and nearly all for the time in question) has been lost.

Apples to Asia. During the 1930s, Nick Borina (far right, top photo) was one of the leaders in developing a market for California apples in Asia. These photos depict visitors to the Borina operations identified as "Mr. and Mrs. Wing," presumably from the Wing Coffee Company of Honolulu, which distributed Borina apples throughout Asia.

The first payment from Wing Coffee Company recorded in the Borina ledgers was on October 10, 1929. A little more than a year later, in November 1930, Wing made four payments to Borina, totaling $2,825.86, or 13.37 percent of Borina's receipts for that month. Payments from Wing Coffee Company came in steadily until the ledger ended in 1936, and sometimes they accounted for nearly 30 percent of Borina's monthly revenues. And it would appear that the Borina-Wing alliance was highly beneficial to both sides. On December 8, 1932, the Honolulu *Star-Bulletin* reported that Wing Coffee Company had moved its wholesale fruit department "across the street from the main store into more spacious quarters."

Ledger entries also indicate that as the decade went on, Borina was selling fruit through a number of other brokers known to be dealing with the Asian market. These included the aforementioned John Demartini Co.; Getz Bros. & Co. of San Francisco, which represented the Pacific Fruit Exchange in Asian markets; and Sunset Produce and Royal Produce. Other records show Borina shipping by truck directly to steamships, docked in San Francisco, that sailed the Pacific routes to Hawaii and Asia, including the *Lurline* and *Celtic Star.*

A critical issue in shipping to Asia was presenting the product for the market. One long-time apple grower recalls that Borina's apples were individually wrapped within boxes sent to Asian customers, which would be consistent with the question of how to make the sale of a single apple as luxury item. Some concerns that shipped to Asia developed special fruit-box labels with Asian themes, such as the Ricksha Apples brand of the Central Coast Marketing Assn. A search of local fruit-label files turned up no Borina labels with Asian themes, nor did a search of several online vendors of fruit labels. (But there is one,

Diamond Head, with a Hawaiian theme.) What Borina's apple boxes looked like when they arrived in Asia remains unknown.

By the end of the 1930s, the extent of Borina's involvement in Asia was indicated in a throw-away line in a letter written September 27, 1939, by Mary Ann to June, who was at Stanford at the time. "We won't have any more apples going out now until we get Honolulu orders at the end of the week," Mary Ann wrote, "so that means no packing, and things will be still more dull around here."

■

THE BORINA FAMILY wasn't much for keeping written personal records; if any of them kept a diary or a journal, it is long since lost, and much of what is now known about them is through the recollections of others and a handful of newspaper clippings. But for one short period, there is a fairly good written record. When Mary Ann and June were at Stanford, they were there together only for spring semester. June attended during the normal academic year, while Mary Ann skipped the fall semester to stay home and help with the family apple business, then went to school spring semester, and in the summer, when June was home. During the school terms when the sisters were separated, they wrote numerous letters to each other, and some of that correspondence has survived and is on file with the Borina Foundation.

The letters, covering a period from July 1938 to June 1941, shed light on a number of subjects and give a sense of the feisty characters of the Borina daughters in their early adulthood. Parts of them are worth quoting verbatim for those reasons. For instance, it turns out that Mary Ann and June were both fairly interested in sports (as fans, anyway). June wrote a long letter describing the thrilling ending of a

Stanford-USC football game she saw, in which Stanford won on a Frankie Albert touchdown pass in the last minutes. In October 1939, when the team was struggling, Mary Ann wrote:

We've been listening to all the games. What in the heqq [sic] happened to Stanford anyway? If I were they, I'd just cancel all their schedule and put the guys to do a little school work. They're bum at school work and lousier on the gridiron, eh? Do you know that the Yanks won the World Series? I listened to the game today, and if you want a thrill, boy, you should listen to one of these baseball games. Beats football all to pieces.

A November 6, 1939, letter from Mary Ann gives an insight as to how Nick was regarded by fellow growers:

Crowe was here today and brought a bill with a stamp on it that says all bills due & payable & delinquent, etc. 7 days after presentation. Pa saw it & did his ears burn. (We haven't paid for two weeks.) Pa told me to get that check book and write him a check !Q*!!*&. Crowe said that's all right, Nick. The bookkeeper made a mistake. You know we only put that stamp on bills to these fellows we aren't sure of.

Somewhat surprisingly, given how she ended up professionally, June found law school tough sledding at first. In an October 17, 1940, letter to Mary Ann, she wrote:

I am writing this in between my Contracts and Sales courses & I have to make it snappy. J____ C____ [dashes hers] but Contracts gives me nightmares. Half the time I don't know what Hurlbut [the professor] is talking about, and I don't believe he knows either! Sales isn't half as bad, but it's bad enough.

Her letters contained numerous references to working hard, such as this, dated May 5, 1941:

Am really buckling down to work. Got up at 5 this morning & studied like a fiend. It sure is swell to work at that time of morning, because everything is so quiet.

But, as indicated by the paragraph that immediately followed, it wasn't all work:

Did you listen to Jack Benny last night? I thought his violin solo was perfect — or was it he playing?

The sisters could also tease each other, as shown in this excerpt from a February 1941 letter by June, commenting on work being done on the family home:

I'm glad the house is coming along so well. I'll be home this Saturday to do a little heckling & criticizing — you know me. Oh, so you'll bounce me out on my ear! Listen, toots, if I know my law (which I don't) that would give me a cause of action vs. you, but let's skip it now.

And in a couple of the letters, June, a lifelong Republican, passed along some digs at President Franklin D. Roosevelt. In one, she enclosed a letter supposedly addressed to FDR, signed by one "Bobby Student," making light of the military draft, which had just been reinstituted. In a May 5, 1941, letter she enclosed an underlined clipping of a letter to the Stanford *Daily* from another student, defending Charles Lindbergh (then one of the leading voices of America's isolationists) and caustically attacking Roosevelt.

By 1941, after Mary Ann had graduated and when June was in law school, Lucy was ill. Many of the letters from Mary Ann to June contained reports on Lucy's situation and how the day had been going for her. On February 8, 1941, Mary Ann wrote:

Ma is feeling as good as expected. The medicine is helping a lot. The doc will be here again to check up. Will write you what he says.

A letter dated March 2 ends:

Well, I guess it's time for me to sign off so that I can get up early and give ma her breakfast. She's got a good appetite, so I guess that's one sign that she must be feeling pretty good. I think if she has a good rest and keeps pretty quiet for a few weeks, she'll be OK.

A letter to June dated June 9 concludes:

Ma had a pretty good day today—that is, when it comes to treats. Along with your letter, I took her a nice delicious quart of ice cream, because it was pretty hot. So with letter in one hand and spoon in the other, she really had a treat.

Two days later, on June 11, 1941, while walking in the Borina orchards on Riverside Road, Lucy suffered a heart attack and was rushed by ambulance to the hospital, where she died. She was 53 years old.

■

LUCY'S DEATH CAME near the end of a period of several years of travail for the Borina family and its apple business. The outbreak of war in Europe in 1939 had effectively cut off those markets, which were part of the business, though it's hard to say how much. Six months after Lucy's death the attack on Pearl Harbor did the same for Asian markets, though U.S. military purchases subsequently made up for some of that.

For most of his professional life, Nick Borina pretty much stayed out of court. Up to the late 1930s, he was involved in only a handful of lawsuits, mostly involving routine payments, and most settled fairly quickly. But at the end of the decade he was a defendant in two more significant actions — one affecting his relations with other growers and one with his own family.

In the former, the Watsonville Apple Growers and Packers Assn., a successor to the group formed in the 1920s (with Nick as one of the founding directors) sued him for allegedly selling part of his apple crop outside the association. Records on file at the Santa Cruz County Superior Court offices show no resolution, and the case (surprisingly, given the prominence of the people involved) wasn't reported in local newspapers at the time it was filed. But it is a fact that the association ceased to exist by the late 1940s, while the Borina apple business was still a thriving concern then.

The second, more personal lawsuit was of a type sadly not uncommon in successful families. On January 3, 1939, Martin Borina, Nick's brother, and Martin's wife, Stella, sued Nick, claiming he had violated an oral agreement to set aside part of their wages toward the purchase of a property. Nick vehemently denied the allegations and fought the lawsuit aggressively for more than three years. Finally, a confidential settlement, details unknown, was reached in the spring of 1942.

A couple of oblique references to legal matters in Mary Ann's letters to June suggest that the lawsuits were a drain on the family. In one, she wrote of a deposition (no indication for which case) that had to be postponed owing to Lucy's illness. Certainly the loss of a life partner, serious legal entanglements, and the loss of a major business market would put anyone to a test. Still, Nick continued to work and the business continued to be a going concern.

In 1945 Nick was diagnosed with cancer,[10] but was treated and was able to keep working on at least a part-time basis. In December of 1949 he was hospitalized following a heart attack and died a few days later on December 19, one day before his 60th birthday.

Mary Ann Borina (Radovich). After her father's death, she took over
day-to-day management of the family farming operations, in consulta-
tion with her sister. Her focus on acquiring good farm land enabled
the business to weather changes in the agricultural industry.

———⊷∘⊶———

Chapter 4

Mary Ann (Borina) Radovich

When Mary Ann Borina enrolled at Stanford in 1936, she had an idea that she wanted to become a schoolteacher, and toward that end she majored in psychology and studied political science. She apparently never viewed her college education as preparation for entering the family business. Three decades later, in an interview for the UC-Santa Cruz Oral History Project, she was asked if she ever studied business in college, and her answer was a single word: "No."

In that interview, there also occurred the following exchange between Mary Ann and interviewer Meri Knaster.

Knaster: At any time in your schooling did you get particular instruction in agriculture?
Mary Ann: No, I didn't feel I needed it.
Knaster: Okay. (laughter)
Mary Ann: (laughter)
Knaster: Did you ever work in any other capacity except with apples. Did you ever hold down any other jobs?
Mary Ann: No, I didn't. I worked just here, at home.

Having worked at her father's side since the age of 14, she learned the business that way and was quickly thrown into it after graduating from college. Her mother died a year after Mary Ann graduated, and with her limited mobility, Mary Ann couldn't replace Lucy in the orchards. But from the accounts of several people who knew the family, she deeply admired her father, who in turn came to rely on her as a pro forma business partner.

"Mary Ann was just like a son to Nick," said one grower who knew the family well.

Following her mother's death, Mary Ann worked closely with her father through the last eight tumultuous years of his life. The outbreak of World War II cut off Borina's Asian shipments — actually nearly all foreign shipments of fruit, she said. Market disruptions went hand in hand with labor disruptions, as men went off to serve. She recalled the situation in the oral history interview:

"When the War started, well, there were many changes. Number one, the labor supply was no longer there. I remember at the time my father had a cold storage, and to do those stacking of boxes inside, there would be teams from Fort Ord. The boys who would volunteer to work would come in and they'd work, that is the ones who could get off. And every night of the week there was a team available. You would sign up for it, and then they would come in and work. The boys from the banks, that worked in the banks, they would sign up for work. A lot of the downtown businesses would have their staffs sign up and then you would draw from those groups."

The improvisational nature of those years, which included women doing work that had previously been the province of men, would likely have provided excellent business training for an alert young woman, such as Mary Ann. When Nick Borina was diagnosed with cancer in 1945, Mary Ann began to take on more of the responsibility of running the business, and by the time he died in 1949, she was by all accounts ready to step in and take over. Nor did she have much choice if the business was to continue, since June was by then well established in her legal career. In the oral history interview, Mary Ann said it really wasn't a decision at all.

"I was just there, and the job was mine, and that's it," she said. Of course my father passed away in 1949, and so there really wasn't much time in between [the cancer diagnosis and his death] to make too many decisions as to whether I would stay or go or what to do ... You just did it because of these other circumstances."

■

MARY ANN WAS 31 when she took over the Borina farming operations and continued to run them until her death more than four decades later. She consulted closely with June during that time, and indeed added M.A. Borina and J. Borina above her father's name on the N.M.B. apple-box label with the eagle on it following Nick's death. But June's involvement, especially after she moved to the Bay Area in 1955, was at a remove, and Mary Ann was running a major farming operation day-to-day in the Pajaro Valley, and probably was one of the few women so situated in the rest of the country as well. In another UC-Santa Cruz oral history, Ray Travers, a longtime apple grower, said that the only two women he knew who had actually run farming operations in the area were Ella Thurwachter in the Beach Road area and Mary Ann. Asked about other women in agriculture by Knaster, Mary Ann replied:

"Well, I guess there have been a few on a small scale, you know, widows and some that have taken over from their parents and then gotten out … you know, kind of on an interim basis. But I don't know of any that have been in as long as I have [nearly 28 years, at the time of the interview]."

For the record, Mary Ann said that she didn't think being a woman in an overwhelmingly male business was any big deal and acknowledged that her having been involved with the family business since an early age may have made her situation different from that of women who got into farming at a later age. There was this exchange in the oral history interview:

Knaster: Did you ever feel that men in the business didn't take you as seriously or deal with you the same as they did with the other people in the business?

Mary Ann: Well, it's possible, but I never looked at it that way, to tell you the truth. I've never thought about it. I've always felt an equal. Well, I didn't go bankrupt so they didn't force me out of business.

Knaster: (laughter)

Mary Ann: (laughter)

Knaster: That's a good observation!

Mary Ann: I've always been told that I think like a man. I think men have always respected my thinking. Maybe they would have liked to have shot me a time or two, when I spoke up and didn't agree with them.

Later in the interview, Knaster raised the question again, in a slightly different way:

Knaster: Do you see any advantages or disadvantages to being the only woman grower?

Mary Ann: In Watsonville?

Knaster: Yes.

Mary Ann: No, I don't see any disadvantages. I don't see any advantages. I think it's strictly a man's world.

Knaster: Is it?

Mary Ann: And you have to learn to play by the rules. I don't think it will ever be a woman's world, and I don't want it to be that way. I don't think women were meant to be the rulers of the world. I don't believe in a matriarchal society (laughter). I still think it's a man's world.

Others who knew her well added a slightly different perspective. John Radin, longtime Watsonville city manager, and a close friend, said, "Being a woman, she thought the men in business were against her, and that drove her to work even harder. I think that drove her more than anything."

John Ivanovich, her longtime next-door neighbor and accountant, recalled her hard-headed business approach in an interview shortly before his death in 2012.

"She was a tough businesswoman, to say the least," Ivanovich said. "If someone else was selling something for four dollars, she wanted five. People liked her, but she had a reputation for being a tough lady."

Radin recalled a situation in the 1960s, when he was then the Finance Officer for the City of Watsonville. The city wanted to acquire a bowling alley so it could be demolished as part of a street realignment project. It was one of the miscellaneous commercial properties the Borinas had acquired over the years, and Radin was assigned to negotiate its purchase from Mary Ann.

Starting life together. Mary Ann Borina and Rado Radovich were married May 15, 1957, and were together 34 years before her death in 1991. She relied on him to run the field operations on the family farms.

"We finally reached an agreement," he said, "but I was scared to death negotiating with her. Mary Ann was a hard person to deal with in a business situation, but she had a heart of gold."

■

MARY ANN'S BUSINESS acumen was put to a test not long after her father died. On an industry-wide basis, apples in Santa Cruz County reached their peak in the 1920s. By the end of World War II apples were beginning a slow but steady decline in acreage and volume, largely owing to competition from the Washington State apple industry, though they remained the county's leading dollar-volume crop into the 1980s. In terms of the Borinas' own operations, Mary Ann needed to adjust to a major shift in the business model.

In his later years Nick Borina had become less of a grower himself and more of a packer and shipper. He was, in essence, a conduit for getting Pajaro Valley apples to the outside world. Structuring the business that way had depended to a large extent on the existence of a profitable Asian market, but within a few years of the end of World War II, it became apparent that the market was gone for the foreseeable future. Japan was devastated and struggling to recover, and China had become Communist and was increasingly closed off to the rest of the world.

Mary Ann and June jointly owned the family properties and consulted on business operations, but it was Mary Ann who ran things day-to-day until her death. In the 1950s she phased out the packing operations and began to focus on acquiring more high quality farm land in the Pajaro Valley.

Bill Locke-Paddon, her attorney in later years, said that Mary Ann had a keen eye for good farm land and was always on the lookout for prime agricultural property. One Pajaro Valley apple grower who knew the family well estimates that she grew the family's farm holdings by 50 percent or more.

"She had what her dad had and went forward from there," he said. "When you buy one piece of land it helps you buy another." He elaborated that revenue from farming operations on a new property could help generate the down payment on the next piece of land, but only for someone who was thrifty and shrewd. "You have to be prepared to save money, and you have to have that money ready when a good piece of land comes available."

In the UC-Santa Cruz oral history interview, Mary Ann said that she had realized apples were no longer a growth industry in Santa Cruz County and that she had structured her holdings to provide a long-term sustainable income from the land. She was, in essence, betting on the long-term utility and value of the area's high quality farm land and figuring that its quality and location would make it continuously valuable, regardless of changes in local crop patterns and farming practices.

That proved to be a wise bet. Fifteen years after her death, Locke-Paddon, who was then administering the family lands, which had then grown to 460 acres, said, "I've been told by people who have observed agriculture around the world that this is some of the best land anywhere for farming, and that there's no reason it can't be farmed for hundreds of years to come."

■

FOR MORE THAN seven years after her father's death, Mary Ann continued to run the day-to-day business of the farm operations herself. On May 15, 1957, she married Rado Radovich, who in America had taken the name Rafael, and he became both her partner in life and in business. The wedding took place at St. Catherine of Siena Church in Burlingame at 10:30 a.m., with her sister, June, serving as matron of honor and her brother-in-law, Robert Schnacke, as best man. A reception followed immediately afterward at the Villa Hotel in San Mateo, then at 4:30 p.m. the newlyweds boarded a ship that would take them to their honeymoon in Hawaii. Fittingly, it was the *S.S. Lurline*, one of the steamers that, two decades earlier, had regularly carried Nick Borina's apples to Asia.

Mary Ann was 38 at the time of the wedding and Radovich was nine years younger. In May of 1953, he had made a daring escape from Communist Yugoslavia, setting out to cross the Adriatic with two friends in a 13-foot rowboat, then arriving in America a couple of years later through a letter of recommendation from Watsonville's Resetar family. In the course of research, several stories were put forth as to how they met, and there is no way of telling which, if any, is true. The common thread among them, however, is that the two were introduced by friends, either at an event or some common gathering place. He had been in the country for barely two years when they married, and according to a number of people who knew him, his grasp of English at the time was somewhere between severely limited and nonexistent. Mary Ann, however, had grown up speaking Croatian with her parents, so they had no problem communicating.

After the honeymoon, the couple returned to Watsonville and made their home at 537 East Third Street (now Beach Street). Mary Ann's aunt, Kate Arbanas, lived in a cottage behind the house and prepared most of the family meals. Radovich immediately went to work in the family business. Mary Ann handled business operations, first from the office at the packing house, and later out of her home. Radovich was the field man, working in the orchards and overseeing the land, learning English and Spanish as he went.

In the UC-Santa Cruz oral history interview, conducted after they had been married 20 years, Mary Ann went into some detail about how she and Rado worked together:

Mary Ann: Of course I'm somewhat out of it [overseeing the farm operations] now and I'm not in it as I was before, because my husband is doing a lot of the work that I used to do.

Knaster: When did he start doing that?

Mary Ann: Oh, when we were married … We kind of split the work then. (laughter). We decided it would make a more harmonious existence.

Knaster: Not both of you being out there (laughter).

Mary Ann: In the same place (laughter) at the same time … But we still talk everything over, and I've given up working with the help. He's a lot better to work with people than I am. I recognize my limitations. I find that men will not always accept orders from the women.

Knaster: Even if you're the boss?

Mary Ann: Well, I shouldn't put it that way. They will accept orders from me; that is, the ones who have been with us, who are permanent workers, but a lot of the migrants don't regularly accept it

… Just on general principle, it seems to work better when the workers get their instructions from a man.

Knaster: Was your husband experienced in apples before he started helping in the business?

Mary Ann: No, we just kind of learned things as we went along. Actually he was trained for restaurant work. He was a hotel manager in Newark. But it's not difficult to learn. I think the basic thing that is required is an ability to work with people, and when you can work with people, there's no problem. Because people are the same whether you are working in a hotel, or whether you're working in an orchard, or whether you're working anywhere else — it's the same thing. You have to know people. You have to understand people. You have to be aware of their problems, willing to listen to their problems. He's very good at that.

One of the defining symbols of their working relationship, according to former City Manager Radin, was a two-way radio, which, in pre-cell phone days, allowed them to stay in close communication. "She used it all the time," Radin said. "Rado was always taking a ribbing about that."

As time passed, theirs appeared to be a happy marriage. Mary Ann said that marrying Rado, who was so closely connected with the old country, led her to become more reconnected with it herself. Members of his family came over to America for month-long stays, Radin said, and as things loosened up in Communist Yugoslavia, Mary Ann and Rado made a number of trips there.

They entertained at their home, and Mary Ann, who had no children, particularly enjoyed hosting baby and bridal showers. She didn't like to cook, though, and Radin and Ivanovich both said that when she was hosting them for dinner, she was likely to take everyone out to a restaurant, rather than cooking at home.

Mary Ann was active in the community in a variety of ways. She supported numerous charitable causes, especially those involving children, and was a member of the American Association of University Women. She served on the Santa Cruz County Planning Commission and was a board member of the Community Foundation of Santa Cruz County in its early years.

For more than 30 years, she and Rado worked to keep the family farming operations a vibrant concern. "They worked hard all year long," said neighbor Ivanovich. "They may have taken a two-week vacation once a year, but that was about it." Radin said that when they did travel, they loved it and did it right. He and his wife, Clara, accompanied them on a number of overseas trips, and he has many fond memories.

"They were fun to travel with," he recalled. "When you went with Mary Ann, you went first cabin." As an example, he cited a trip to Auckland, New Zealand. Because of the lingering effects of Mary Ann's polio, she often rented a car with a driver, so in Auckland the four of them saw the city from the same Rolls Royce limousine that had transported Queen Elizabeth on her most recent visit. During a visit to Sydney, Australia, Rado looked up one of his boat mates from the escape from Yugoslavia. "There turned out to be a tight Croatian colony in the city," Radin said. "It kind of reminded me of old Watsonville, when the area from Kearney and Rodriguez, Fifth and Sixth streets was all Slav."

In late 1991, not long after returning from a trip to Australia, Radin went to visit the Radoviches and found Mary Ann quite ill, but resisting her husband's entreaties that she see a doctor. Radin said he finally prevailed upon her to go to Dominican Hospital, and when they got there, he offered to check her in. "She said she'd do it herself," he recalled. "It was one of the last things she ever did."

Several days later, on December 19, 1991, Mary Ann Radovich died at the hospital of complications from pneumonia at the age of 73.

June Borina (Schnacke). In 1947, at the age of 27, she became District Attorney of Santa Cruz County, the first female DA in California history. Watsonville Police Chief Frank Osmer said of her, "She was very good, very efficient."

Chapter 5

June (Borina) Schnacke

In September 1942, a year after her mother's death, June Borina graduated from Stanford Law School at the age of 22. Shortly thereafter, even though suffering from a temporarily disabling injury, she took the California Bar Examination lying flat on her back and passed it. A female lawyer was an anomaly in that era, but with the war under way, she got an opportunity to practice law and made the most of it.

At the time, the district attorney of Santa Cruz County was Stephen Wyckoff, of the same family that had leased an orchard to Martin Secondo, June's grandfather, four decades earlier. Wyckoff was running the Santa Cruz DA's office by himself, with longtime deputy John McCarthy running the office in Watsonville. Needing help, Wyckoff offered June a position as deputy, and she joined the office in February 1943. After interviewing her a decade later, the Watsonville *Register-Pajaronian*[11] described what it was like back then:

"Miss Borina can recall the days when she first came to work for Santa Cruz County, when there were not more than a half-dozen deputies in the sheriff's office. There were seven employees in the county welfare department. There was no road commissioner. There was plenty of room, and some to spare, for every county department and employee in the old courthouse and the 'huge' annex built with WPA money in 1936. Santa Cruz County was still a cow county."

Ceremonial duties. As District Attorney, June handled mostly civil cases, oversaw a small department, and performed ceremonial duties like this sheriff's swearing-in (date unknown).

COURTESY OF COVELLO & COVELLO PHOTOGRAPHY

Gender first. Two months into her job as District Attorney, June prosecuted her first criminal trial, facing off against defense attorney Barbara Cochrane in a bad-check case. It was the first trial involving two female lawyers in Santa Cruz County history; June won.

Troubled successor. Charles Moore (right, holding book, with Watsonville Police Chief Frank Osmer) defeated June in a nasty 1954 race for District Attorney. Less than a year later, he was under indictment for misconduct in office and resigned rather than facing trial.

In criminal terms, it was a quiet county. Santa Cruz was a small beach town, and Watsonville was a small farm town, albeit with a disreputable side. Its houses of prostitution (along with some gambling operations) had earned it a reputation in Central California as "Sin City," and during World War II, it was off limits to soldiers at nearby Fort Ord. The city police department managed, rather than challenged, the vice situation, and arrests and prosecutions were rare. As June later told attorney Austin Comstock, who was interviewing her for a legal history of Santa Cruz County, "We used to do a lot of winking at some things around." After the War, Watsonville quietly and substantively clamped down on vice activities, but its reputation lived on well into the 1950s and came back to hurt June politically later in her career.

According to the *Register-Pajaronian*,[11] criminal matters at the time June joined the office took up only 20 percent of its time. The district attorney also served as county counsel, advising the county on all legal matters, mostly civil. This was the area where, by all accounts, she shined. As the story went on to report:

"As a deputy, Miss Borina worked out the massive school reorganization program that resulted, in 1946, in the present Freedom and Salsipuedes school districts. Later, as district attorney, she led the county schools office, San Lorenzo Valley and the embattled Santa Cruz high school district through the storms that eventually settled with the unification of the San Lorenzo Valley school district.

"She was legal advisor in the organization of the Boulder Creek, Ben Lomond, Opal Cliffs and La Selva Recreation districts. She put through the formation of fire districts in Freedom, Salsipuedes, Felton, Live Oak, Branciforte, La Selva Beach and the Watsonville west side."

In addition, she spent hours on the legalities of the formation of the City of Capitola in 1949 and did the legal work for the county on the expansion of Highway 1 after the war.

Wyckoff was re-elected district attorney in 1946, but before he had served even a year of his first term decided to resign and go into private practice. The Santa Cruz *Sentinel* reported that he cited the "absurdly low" salary of $3,300 per year as the reason for moving into a more lucrative position with his own firm, and that the county Grand Jury was recommending an increase to $4,800 per year. By law, the Santa Cruz County Board of Supervisors would be responsible for appointing a replacement to serve out Wyckoff's term.

McCarthy, the long-term deputy in Watsonville also applied for the job, and June later said a part of her felt he should have received the appointment. But she had been working closely with the Board of Supervisors for four years and had earned their respect. The board also wanted a district attorney from Santa Cruz, and June had moved there to be closer to her job, while McCarthy had said he might have difficulty reconciling the DA's job in Santa Cruz with his Watsonville interests. June also had endorsements from the county's Republican Women club and the San Lorenzo Valley Business and Professional Women's club, as well as from a number of private individuals who wrote letters on her behalf. She was appointed on a unanimous vote in May 1947 and took charge when Wyckoff's resignation went into effect June 30. It was a historic appointment, inasmuch as she became the first female district attorney in the history of California and one of few, if any, in the nation at the time. "I was in the right place at the right time," she told the *Register-Pajaronian* decades later.

She gave the formal letter of appointment to her proud father, who put it on the wall of his office in the packing shed and showed it to almost everyone who came in over the last two years of his life. "He'd bore people," she later told the *Register-Pajaronian*, laughing as she said it.

McCarthy at first took June's appointment personally and resigned as deputy district attorney in Watsonville. J. Frank Coakley, Alameda County District Attorney, who knew June through the state district attorneys' association, assigned two of his young prosecutors to Santa Cruz County to help keep the office going for a few months before McCarthy relented and asked for his job back. June took him back, saying that as far as she was concerned he'd never left.

Following her appointment, June served three years, then ran for the office unopposed in 1950. As district attorney, she earned high marks from nearly everyone. Frank Osmer, who was appointed Watsonville police chief at around the same time June was appointed DA, later told the *Register-Pajaronian*, "She was very good, very efficient. There was no question about gender ... You couldn't tell the difference from her predecessor."

Sam McNeely, who served as Santa Cruz City Councilman and Mayor, said, "We know the importance of integrity in the district attorney's office, and we know that that is what we've had during June's term in office."

Her former boss, Wyckoff, a few years removed from the job, later said, "That office, now that I am in private practice, gives me a bad time on criminal cases ... I wouldn't respect her or the staff if they didn't make it as difficult as possible."

Perhaps because McCarthy, universally acknowledged to be the best trial attorney in the office, was away at the time, June personally prosecuted her first criminal trial as district attorney less than two months into office. The trial was unusual for another gender-bending first in Santa Cruz County history. It was the first jury trial in which both attorneys were female.

June represented the people in prosecuting Claude Sterling of Santa Cruz for bouncing more than $1,300 worth of checks at the Quality Paint Store. Sterling was represented by Barbara Cochrane, who was appointed by the court to represent him and who was believed to have been the first female defense attorney in a criminal case in county history. The criminal-justice system moved a bit more quickly in those days, and the trial lasted only a day, with the jury taking but an hour and a half to find the defendant guilty.

It was unusual for June to handle a trial personally. In administering the office, she tended to take an approach of hiring good people and trusting their judgment. Her former deputies, including Ray Scott, Jim Paxton and Robert Darrow, said she rarely argued a case in court herself and was more of an administrator. Of her relationship with McCarthy, Darrow said in a 2007 interview, "They saw eye to eye, so there wasn't much contact between them. He was pretty much revered by everyone, and she let him run the Watsonville office as he saw fit."

She did, however, according to Scott, emphasize that, especially in criminal cases, a prosecutor should realize the potential impact of a prosecution and be sure there was a solid case before filing charges.

Years later, June told Austin Comstock that even though she was the state's first female district attorney, she never felt like a trail-blazer, and that although she felt she did her job competently, she was naïve about what she was up against as a woman. Comstock's notes of the interview read, "It was at a time when male dominance of the profession, particularly dealing with police and crime matters [was so entrenched], that I think as she looks back she figures she was truly naïve, but she nevertheless persevered."

The male dominance of the profession and the attitudes that prevailed at the time are hard to fathom today. A 1952 photograph, taken by Covello & Covello, of the Santa Cruz County Bar Association, shows 29 clean-shaven men in suits and ties, with June, seated at the end of the second row, the only woman in the photo. (See p. 87)

And the double standard shown toward the handful of women in the public view could be seen in news stories of the time, which regularly referred to June as "Miss Borina," while referring to male attorneys and public figures by last name only. A 1948 article on the society page of the *Register-Pajaronian* began, "California's most attractive district attorney doubled as guest speaker and guest of honor at Monday evening's meeting of the Optimist Club at the Eagles Hall." After the bad-check trial, the Santa Cruz *Sentinel-News* published a front page photo of June and Barbara Cochrane with the caption: "Both these Portias appear pleased, although District Attorney June Borina (seated) has the greater cause as she won her first conviction in her first jury trial Wednesday ..."

As a single woman in a position of considerable public responsibility, June was also driven to be circumspect about personal matters. "She never discussed personal affairs," her deputy, Darrow, said. "She felt they didn't affect who she was or her operation of the office." The only thing on the record in that regard was her comment to Comstock a year before her death. "She said there was not a bar in Watsonville she could go to as a young, single female, but there were a couple in

Santa Cruz where she was able to go without drawing lots of stares and attention," Comstock wrote.

There was one more thing about June as district attorney. Everyone who knew her at the time agreed that she had no instinct for politics. "She wasn't a politician in the sense of attending events or shaking hands," Darrow said. "She was very low-key on political matters. She put more emphasis on being a good district attorney than on being a politician." Her indifference to politics, coupled with being a woman in what was definitely a man's profession at the time, figured heavily when she ran for re-election as district attorney in 1954.

By that time, as Santa Cruz County had participated modestly in California's postwar growth, the office had grown, and June was presiding over three deputies in Santa Cruz — Scott, Paxton and Darrow. Vice operations in Watsonville had by then been substantively curtailed, and the county as a whole was a low-crime, small-town and rural area. Despite those positive factors, June found herself running in a contested election for the first time in her career.

Her challengers were John Barber, a local attorney who had been practicing in the county since 1949, and Charles L. Moore, Jr., like June a Stanford law graduate, who had moved to the county from San Francisco in the fall of 1953. Given the advantage of incumbency, a solid record in office, and the nearly unanimous support of the county's civic leaders, June was widely regarded as the favorite, with Barber seen as her most serious challenger. Heading into the June primary, the race attracted nearly no media coverage.

That worked to the advantage of Moore, who showed an intuitive understanding of politics that June and Barber couldn't begin to match. In 1954 the first television station in the Monterey Bay area — NBC affiliate KSBW in Salinas — began to broadcast, and Moore grasped the power of the new medium. With the help of contributions from members of the Santa Cruz Taxpayers Association, which was vituperatively critical of nearly every elected official, he bought considerable air time to make a name and presence for himself. Aided by his youthful good looks (he was 27 at the time) he quickly developed a strong camera presence. Three months before he died in December of 2007, Moore told an interviewer that KSBW had offered him a job as a newscaster if politics didn't pan out for him.

He also campaigned openly and behind the scenes on a platform of cleaning up Watsonville, which he portrayed as a cesspool of vice and organized crime. Publicly, he repeatedly made strongly worded allegations to that effect and waved off demands that he provide any proof of what he was saying. Quietly, he circulated among churches in Santa Cruz and the northern part of the county, enlisting the support of ministers to whom he made a promise that he would clean up what he called rampant vice and crime in Watsonville. A number of the clergy advocated for him with their parishioners. Finally, Moore also played the gender card, running a print advertisement with the headline, "Why Send a Girl on a Man's Errand? Elect Moore District Attorney."

In the June primary election, Moore and June ran neck and neck (he led her by 29 votes out of 24,000 cast), with Barber a distant third, and the race went into a runoff at the November general election. In her native Watsonville, where she and her family were known and respected, June handily outpolled Moore and the other candidates. But three quarters of the electorate lived outside the Pajaro Valley, and Moore carried those voters.

The local establishment (including the media) belatedly began to take the election and Moore's campaign seriously, but it was too late. The *Register-Pajaronian* and Santa Cruz *Sentinel* ran in-depth articles that raised numerous questions about Moore. Local elected officials and civic leaders rallied to June's support. Don Grunsky, the area's popular Republican State Senator broke a longstanding policy against endorsements in local races to support June. Days before the election, the *Register-Pajaronian* endorsed her in an editorial that mercilessly dissected Moore's problems and ended with the words:

> Mr. Moore has not been forthright on the issue of organized crime. He lacks the necessary experience to handle either the criminal or civil work of the office. His record in the courts here is not imposing.
>
> Mr. Moore's election, we are very much afraid, would be a source of regret to the people of Santa Cruz County long before the four-year term ended. We can't afford to take the chance.

None of it mattered. At the November general election, Charles Moore was elected district attorney with 62 percent of the vote. The county's civic leaders were stunned, as were all those working in the district attorney's office. Half a century later, Darrow recalled, "We were proud of our office and thought we were doing an excellent job. We tried to convey that to the public, and we failed miserably."

The *Register-Pajaronian* editorial, however, proved prophetic. Nine months into office, Moore was in trouble as revelations emerged that his leading campaign contributor had, in essence, been collecting protection money from operators of pinball machines, which were considered gambling devices, saying he would use his influence with Moore to see that they weren't prosecuted. Edmund G. "Pat" Brown, the state attorney general and later governor assigned two of his top deputies to investigate, and they convened a grand jury that indicted Moore for willful and corrupt misconduct in office.

In January of 1956, after just more than a year in office, Moore resigned rather than face trial on the charges. Some members of the Santa Cruz County Board of Supervisors discreetly contacted June to see if she would be interested in a reappointment to her old job, but she declined. By then she had moved on.

In August 1955, June, who was well regarded in state legal circles, was hired at the U.S. Attorney's Office in San Francisco. It was there, at the age of 35, that she met a co-worker who became the love of her life and her husband for nearly four decades.

Robert H. (Bob) Schnacke (pronounced Shh-KNOCK-ee) was a native San Franciscan and a graduate of Lowell High School and Hastings School of Law ('38). Six years older than June, he worked briefly in private practice after graduation, then served as a special agent for the U.S. Army's Counterintelligence Corps during World War II. After several years in private practice, Schnacke, a Republican, was hired as head of the criminal division of the U.S. Attorney's Office after Dwight D. Eisenhower was elected president and named Lloyd Burke to head the San Francisco U.S. Attorney's office.

Aside from the fact that they worked at the same office and would have come into contact with each other, no one seems to know exactly how they met, but they became engaged in June of 1956 and were married Friday September 7 of that year. The ceremony took place at St. Peter and Paul's Catholic Church in San Francisco, with Father Gabriel, former director of St. Francis School for Boys in Watsonville officiating. Mary Ann was June's maid of honor, and many people from the U.S. Attorney's office were in attendance.

After a month-long honeymoon in the West Indies, the couple returned to California, taking up residence in San Francisco, then moving to Hillsborough, south of the City, a few years later. June continued working at the U.S. Attorney's office until 1962, when she resigned her legal position to devote her time to marriage and community work (as well as maintaining an involvement, with her sister, in the Watsonville farming operations).

Robert Schnacke and June Borina met in the U.S. Attorney's office in San Francisco, married in 1956, and were together almost 38 years.

Bob Schnacke went on to enjoy a distinguished and successful legal career. At some point after the marriage, he left the U.S. Attorney's office to work in private practice. In 1968, Governor Ronald Reagan appointed him Superior Court Judge in San Francisco. In 1970, Congress passed an omnibus judicial bill, creating a significant number of new federal judgeships, and Schnacke was appointed by President Richard Nixon to a new opening on the U.S. District Court in San Francisco.

Federal District Judge Samuel Conti, born in 1922, was appointed to the bench at the same time as Schnacke, and the two men went on to become close friends. "We were both Republicans in San Francisco, if you can imagine what that means," Conti said in a 2012 phone interview. Of his colleague, he added:

"He was a very, very good judge, quite well respected. He handled the calendar quickly and had a no-nonsense approach. He really enjoyed his work; he really loved being a judge."

In Schnacke's obituary, the San Francisco *Chronicle* wrote, "He built a reputation as a strong trial judge with a conservative legal philosophy. Armed with a wry wit and sarcasm to offset a sometimes gruff demeanor, he enjoyed taking an active part in trials, often questioning witnesses from the bench."

He handled a number of well publicized cases, including the criminal trial of Steven Psinakis, who was acquitted of illegal transport of explosives in connection with his role as a leader of the insurgency against Philippine strongman Ferdinand Marcos. In other famous cases, Judge Schnacke ruled that an employer's English-only policy for workplace language was discriminatory and that news photographers could be banned from executions in California on the ground that they might constitute a security threat.

Attorney Bill Locke-Paddon, who represented the Borina family in many of its business and estate matters, said that June was deeply committed to supporting Bob's legal career both by taking care of domestic matters and by providing Schnacke with a keen legal mind to talk to after work.

They were by all accounts devoted to each other and did a great deal of traveling together, sometimes taking their pet German shepherd along on trips within the U.S., and sometimes leaving the dog at home for the neighbors' children to pet-sit in exchange for postcards and postage stamps. Much of their travel was in connection with the judge's job, which called on him to hold court across American holdings in the Pacific Rim.

Judge Conti said he often dined with June and Bob at judicial conferences and from time to time in the ordinary course of things. When he went to the Schnackes for dinner, June typically cooked, but more often, he said, the Schnackes would take him to dinner at their country club.

Getting to know the couple over the years, Conti said, he came to realize June was true to her upbringing. "June really loved her parents and didn't want to do anything that would reflect badly on them," he said. "Like her parents, she had a deep respect for the land and wanted to maintain the family holdings," he said.

June continued to be involved with the family farming operations, though Mary Ann did the day-to-day work. In 1958 June and Bob were pictured in the *Register-Pajaronian*, inspecting the ruins of the family cold storage plant, which had been destroyed by fire. After Mary Ann's death in 1991, June assumed oversight responsibility for the farming operations and came to Watsonville on a regular basis.

But after giving up the practice of law, her time was largely taken up with volunteer work in the Bay Area. She served on the boards of the American Association of University Women and the Medical Missions Auxiliary, was involved with Republican groups, served as a docent at the M.H. DeYoung Memorial Museum, and was a supporter and frequenter of the San Francisco Opera and Symphony.

After Bob died of a heart attack in June 1994 at the age of 80, she created, in his memory, a judicial externship scholarship at Hastings College of Law. As a judge, Bob had engaged law students as externs (students connected with the court and working for it, but not officially employed) on a regular basis and had come to feel that it was an excellent way for law students to broaden and expand upon their classroom education.

The Judge Robert H. Schnacke Scholarships were awarded to as many as five students a year in the amount of $5,000 per student. Students were chosen based on both financial need and overall academic achievement in law school. When the scholarships were first given, a year after Bob's death, the law school magazine characterized the Schnacke contribution as "one of the most generous gifts available to Hastings students." June worked actively on the scholarships and was a regular participant at the scholarship luncheons sponsored by Hastings.

In good health to all appearances, June continued her community work and management of the family farms through the 1990s. But like her mother and father, she eventually succumbed to a sudden heart attack. She was stricken in her Burlingame home and died June 5, 2000, at the age of 80, six years to the day after the death of her beloved husband. With her passing, the Borina family line came to an end, but in her last years, June had taken steps to ensure that the Borina family name would live on.

COURTESY OF COVELLO & COVELLO PHOTOGRAPHY

Santa Cruz County Bar Association. In this group photo from 1952, June (far right, second row) was the only woman. In her re-election campaign two years later, her challenger ran an ad with the headline: "Why Send a Woman on a Man's Errand?"

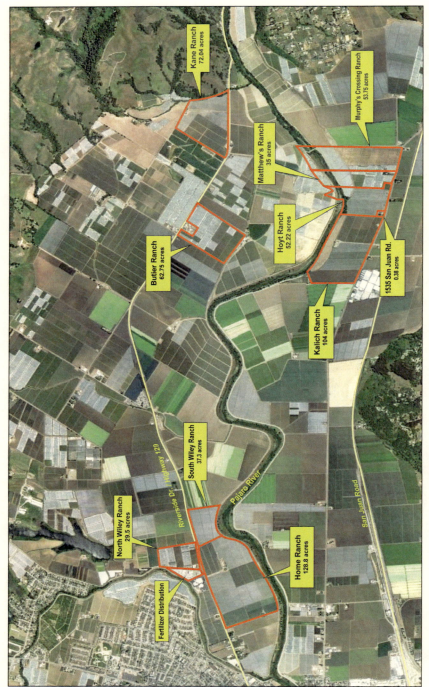

Kane Ranch
72.04 acres

Murphy's Crossing Ranch
53.75 acres

Matthew's Ranch
35 acres

Butler Ranch
62.75 acres

Hoyt Ranch
52.22 acres

1535 San Juan Rd.
0.38 acres

Kalich Ranch
104 acres

South Wiley Ranch
37.3 acres

North Wiley Ranch
29.5 acres

Riverside Dr., Highway 129

Pajaro River

San Juan Road

Fertilizer Distribution

Home Ranch
128.8 acres

The Borina Properties. Land owned by the Borina Foundation is outlined in this NASA photograph. Because these farming lands are protected by conservation easements held by the Land Trust of Santa Cruz County, they serve as a buffer against growth by the city of Watsonville (upper left) on to the prime farmland along the Pajaro River.

MAP LAYOUT COURTESY OF CASSIDY TURLEY

Chapter 6

The Borina Foundation

Following the death of her sister, Mary Ann, June Borina Schnacke spent much of the last decade of her life tending to the family properties, dealing with estate matters, and thinking deeply about what she wanted to leave behind after she died.

"To me it seemed that she didn't want the legacy of what her father and mother had built to go away," said her goddaughter Sheila Burke. "The land was important to her; the family was important to her, and she really turned all her attention to crafting a legacy for the community that would reflect that."

The process of considering that legacy took years and culminated in June's signing, on May 28, 1998, a will that dramatically changed the terms of her estate. Up to that point she had planned on leaving most of it to the University of California Medical Center. The new will, signed just two years before June's death, directed that the bulk of the estate, excluding several specific bequests, be distributed to the Borina Foundation, to be created in memory of the family. The purpose of the Foundation was to make charitable contributions in the greater Pajaro Valley area.

In July 2002 the Borina Foundation came into being, and in the decade since has made significant and wide-ranging contributions to nonprofit organizations in Santa Cruz County. But the path leading to its creation was anything but smooth.

■

PROBLEMS WITH THE Borina family holdings began not long after Mary Ann died. She had ordered a new will drawn up in the year before her death but had not signed it, which meant that her property would have been disposed of under the terms of Mary Ann's most recent will, signed in 1973. That will, however, was challenged by her husband, Rafael Radovich, who filed two lawsuits in connection with the estate, claiming that he had unfairly been denied his share of community property under a prenuptial agreement and that Mary Ann's attorneys had been negligent in processing the second will. A divided jury ruled 9-3 in his favor in the community property suit, and the other suit was eventually thrown out of court. Radovich lived in Watsonville for more than a decade after the lawsuits were decided, then moved to Croatia in 2005. He died June 29, 2008.

The loss of her beloved husband of 38 years in 1994 left June with no living family members, an obligation to tend to the charitable interests her husband had supported over the years, and the sole responsibility for planning for the future of the Borina farming operations. It was around this time, said her attorney, William F. Locke-Paddon, that she began the serious thought and planning for the future that eventually resulted in the unified solution of a single foundation that could address all her concerns.

As set up in June's will, and later established in its articles of incorporation, the Foundation was principally meant to do three things:

• Distribute the earnings of the Borina farm operations to non-profit organizations in Santa Cruz County, with an emphasis on education, historical preservation, and services to the elderly and dying.

• Provide a vehicle for maintaining and preserving the family's farm lands, keeping them in agriculture for as long as possible and providing long-term stability for the tenant farmers and employees.

• Ensure that Judge Schnacke's two principal charitable legacies — to Hastings College of Law for the judicial extern program and St. Anthony's Foundation, which provides basic needs for the poor of San Francisco — were addressed through the set-aside of fixed principal and annual contributions.

Attorney Locke-Paddon was named executor of June's estate and was established as one of the directors of the Borina Foundation. June's goddaughter, Sheila Burke was named as another.

The Borina Foundation received a federal exemption as a charitable foundation in late 2001 and a state exemption in 2002. The first meeting of the board of directors was held in September 2002, and the first charitable grants were made in 2003, following a court order that distributed most of the estate to the Borina Foundation.

Since that time the Foundation has distributed millions of dollars to nonprofit organizations in Santa Cruz County, primarily in the Pajaro Valley. Most of the contributions have been for one-time projects, rather than ongoing expenses.

June was one of the major contributors to the formation of St. Francis Central Coast Catholic High School near Watsonville, giving a million dollars before her death to help establish it. The Foundation subsequently pledged $4 million, payable over a period of years, to fund the Borina Sports Complex at the school. Moreland Notre Dame, the school June first attended at the age of 4, received a $1.2 million grant. Public schools benefited from money to help build playgrounds and support counseling programs.

In the larger community, the Borina Foundation has given to a wide range of organizations, including the YMCA, the Agricultural History Project, the Ed and Jean Kelly Foundation, Second Harvest Food Bank, Loaves and Fishes, Pajaro Valley Shelter Services, Mid-county Senior Center, and the Community Foundation. The Foundation contributed to the new Pajaro Valley Historical Association archive building, and has supported historical research projects, including the writing of *Blossoms into Gold*, and research and printing of *The Slav Community of Watsonville, California: As reported in old newspapers*.

"June and her sister knew the importance of family and of seeking out the needs of the community through volunteerism," Burke said. "She spoke often about responding to the needs of the community and about the importance of recognizing the accomplishments of people in agriculture. When we consider a funding request, we ask ourselves, is this something June would have wanted to do? Is this something that would make her proud ... make her family proud?"

■

BY THE TIME of Mary Ann's death, much of the Borina apple acreage had been converted to row crops, and by the end of 2006 the last remaining apple trees were removed. New crops flourished on the rich farm land, and the Borina Foundation began considering how the land might be protected for farming — if not forever, for as long as humanly possible.

"Every farmer who loves farming hates to give up the land," Locke-Paddon said. "June saw the Foundation as a way of keeping the properties together and taking care of the tenants and their families."

Within a couple of years of the Foundation's incorporation, Locke-Paddon was actively looking for ways to gain permanent protection for the land as farm land. With Burke's support, and the Community Foundation's approval, negotiations commenced with the Land Trust of Santa Cruz County to place a conservation easement on the Borina properties.

The Land Trust is a nonprofit organization dedicated to protecting valuable open-space land, typically by working with the owners to acquire development rights to the land. A conservation easement provides a farmer with both an immediate infusion of cash and a long-term tax break, as the land will be assessed for tax purposes at its value for agriculture, rather than its speculative value if developed. A detailed contract restricts nearly all development on the land, allowing only limited structures clearly related to agricultural purposes.

"Everything that's on the property remains," Locke-Paddon said, "and the right to expand farming operations is retained within defined limits. But the land would be kept in farming, despite the pressure to develop it in the future."

In the case of the Borina property, located on flat, easily buildable land just outside the city of Watsonville and in the shadow of an ever-expanding Silicon Valley, development pressure could have become considerably more intense in coming decades, absent such an agreement. The completion of the conservation easement agreement in late 2008 — following lengthy discussions involving the Land Trust, the Borina Foundation and the Community Foundation (which ultimately inherits the land) — protected more than the Borina properties. By removing those lands from development consideration, the agreement indirectly affected many other farm lands to the east of Watsonville.

"The Borina property is exceptional, not only for its farming value, but for its strategic location," said Land Trust Executive Director Terry Corwin at the time of the agreement. "Securing the development rights to that land will create a significant buffer against the development of the valuable farmland beyond."

The family line established by Nick and Lucy Borina ended with June's death in 2000, but because of the steps she took in the last years of her life, the family legacy will be perpetuated. It will live on in the annual gifts made by the Foundation to the community, and perhaps more importantly in the long-term preservation of the rich, productive land that the Borinas all so loved.

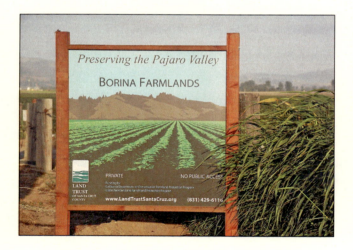

Endnotes

#1 on page 7. Information from a monograph by Dr. Nenad Vekarić of the Croatian Academy of Sciences and Arts in Dubrovnik, Croatia, and printed in a pamphlet entitled, "The Filipović/Borina Family," by Tom Ninkovich, 2004. This pamphlet is in the Borina Estate collection.

#2 on page 8. *Blossoms into Gold*, p. 34. Original source is an article by Dr. Nenad Vekarić entitled "The Influence of Demographic Trends…," published in the quarterly journal, *The History of the Family*, Vol. 1, Issue 4, pp. 461-476; 1996.

#3 on page 8. Ellis Island records for Nikola Borina (ship's manifest) (www.ellisisland.org; July 2013); interpreted by Tom Ninkovich.

#4 on page 9. *Mary Ann Borina Radovich: Croatian Apple Farmer, Watsonville, California, 1918-77*, oral history conducted by Meri Knaster, UC-Santa Cruz Regional Oral History Project. June 1977.

#5 on page 10. *Register-Pajaronian*, June 5, 1968.

#6 on page 10. *The Slav Community of Watsonville, California*, p. 565.

#7 on page 20. *Evening Pajaronian*, April 27, 1907.

#8 on page 29. *The Slav Community of Watsonville, California*, p. 725.

#9 on page 30. This story was told to the author by an elderly resident of the Pajaro Valley who asked not to be quoted by name.

#10 on page 57. *Mary Ann Borina Radovich: Croatian Apple Farmer, Watsonville, California, 1918-77*, oral history conducted by Meri Knaster, UC-Santa Cruz Regional Oral History Project. June 1977.

#11 on pages 73 and 75. *Register-Pajaronian*, October 11, 1954.

———————

Photo Gallery

Clockwise from upper left: ►Mato Borina; his wife, Marija Aguzin; his oldest son, Pasko (standing); son, Mato (left); daughters, Mare (left) and Nike. Nick had left for San Francisco and is not in the photo. ►Martin Secondo, father of the clan. ►Lucy Secondo. ►Lucy Secondo (left) and her friend, Lucy Vlahutin Franusich, dressed in the national dress of Konavle, the region in Dalmatia where they came from (photo taken in San Francisco). ►Kate Secondo Arbanas (left), Lucy Secondo, their mother, Marija Radin Secondo, and Kate's children, Katie and Tommy.

Clockwise from upper left: ▸Wedding of Lucy Secondo Bakich and Nick Borina, both seated (May 13, 1917 in Watsonville). Matron of honor was Lucy's sister, Kate Arbanas. Best man was Nick's brother, Martin Borina. ▸Wedding of Martin Borina and Stella Šapro (July 16, 1922 in Watsonville). ▸Wedding of Mary Borina and John Violich (July 16, 1922 in Watsonville). The last two weddings were a double ceremony. ▸Wedding of Nike Borina and Peter Rajkovich (Feb. 11, 1923). Best man is George Rajkovich; matron of honor is Stella Šapro Borina, Nike's sister.

Clockwise from upper left: ▸Barbecue, Christmas 1920. Note wooden spits of barbecued meat. Nick Borina in middle; Martin Borina and his wife, Stella, on right; Mary Ann and June in front; others unknown. Note U.S. flag. ▸Martin Secondo, his daughters, Lucy (left) and Kate, with guns, his granddaughter, Katie Arbanas. ▸Peter Secondo on his motor bike with Lucy Secondo riding behind. ▸June and Mary Ann Borina (June 1920). Written under this photo in June's scrapbook, in her handwriting is: "Unaccustomed as I am to Public Speaking......!" ▸Peter Radin holding Mary Ann Borina, and Nick Borina looking on (September 1919).

Clockwise from upper left: ▶Nick Borina on right; his brother, Martin in middle; Martin's wife, Stella on left; Mary Ann Borina (left) and June Borina. Christmas 1925.

▶Mary Ann (left) and June Borina.

▶Mary Ann Borina's communion photo.

▶June Borina's communion photo, with her mother and sister.

▶Three sets of first cousins: June Borina (left) and her sister, Mary Ann Borina (right). The Secondo twins, Ben and Rudy, in the middle. Anita Secondo (2nd from left) and her sister, Mildred Secondo (2nd from right).

Clockwise from upper left: ▶The Secondo twins, Ben and Rudy, with their mother, Kate; Mary Ann Borina (left) and June Borina. ▶June and Mary Ann Borina on lawn (November 1931 in Salinas). ▶Mary Ann and June Borina with car (June 1, 1933). ▶Group photo at the Herbert Ranch, Christmas 1937: Nick Borina (right); June Borina standing behind Nick; Mary Ann Borina in middle; note wooden spit with barbecued meat.

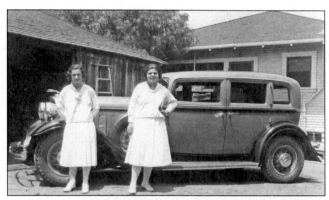

Martin Borina with Mary Ann and June (with reins) on the Riverside Ranch, July 29, 1931. Below, Nick Borina's packing shed, 1930s. It was one of the busiest in the state and considered state-of-the-art.

Photo Credits

*Uncredited photos are from the Borina
Foundation photo collection located at Pajaro
Valley Historical Archives in Watsonville. Photo
credit abbreviations are at end of this list.*

Page / Description / Credit

4. Nick Borina
6. Osojnik, Croatia TN
6. Borina house in Osojnik TN
7. Map of southern Croatia TN
14. Lucy Secondo
16. Martin Secondo
16. Martin, Mary and Lucy Secondo
18. Photos of Secondo siblings
24. Secondo-Borina wedding group
24. (close-up of above)
26. Secondo-Borina wedding photo
28. Lucy Borina and her daughters (2 photos)
28. Nick Borina and his daughters
29. Nick Borina spraying
34. Lucy and Kate, hunting
34. Mary Ann's 1924 birthday party
34. Mary Ann's birthday dress, 1927
34. Mildred and Anita Secondo
38. Moreland Notre Dame class (1933)
38. June's softball team (7th grade, 1931)
38. June with violin
40. June at law school, 1940-41
40. 488 Harvard St., Palo Alto, and Daisy Belle
40. Graduation of law school class, 1942
41. June and Lucy, Donner Pass, 1938
41. June and Mary Ann, San Pedro, Calif., 1936
41. June and friends at Sawmill Flats,
     Washington State, 1940
41. June and Mary Ann at Agua Caliente,
     Mexico, 1935
44. Two Borina apple labels RH
45. Diamond Head label SMB
45. Watsonville Growers' label SMB
45. Borina strawberry label PVHA
50. Chinese visitors (2 photos)
58. Mary Ann Borina
64. Borina-Radovich wedding photo RHC
72. June Borina at desk, as District Attorney
74. Swearing in of Sheriff's staff
74. June Borina, Barbara Cochrane C&C
74. Charles Moore, Frank Osmer RP
84. Borina-Schnacke wedding SMB
87. Bar Association, 1952 C&C

88. Aerial photo of Borina properties CT
94. Borina Farmlands sign LT

Photo Gallery

97. Borina family in Dalmatia MR
97. Mary Radin Secondo, Lucy Secondo, Kate
     Arbanas, Tommy and Katie Arbanas
97. Lucy Secondo (2 portraits)
97. Lucy Secondo, Lucy Franusich, national dress
     of Konavle
98. Secondo-Borina wedding
98. Sapro-Borina wedding
98. Borina-Violich wedding
98. Borina-Rajkovich wedding MR
99. Barbecue (Christmas 1920)
99. Martin Secondo, Lucy Secondo, Kate and
     Katie Arbanas, hunting
99. Peter Secondo, Lucy Secondo, on Pete's
     motor bike
99. June and Mary Ann Borina (June 1920)
99. Peter Radin, Mary Ann and Nick Borina
     (Sept. 1919)
100. Nick, Martin, June, Mary Ann Borina;
      Martin's wife, Stella (Christmas 1925)
100. Mary Ann and June Borina
100. Mary Ann Borina, communion photo
100. June Borina's communion photo
100. June and Mary Ann Borina; Secondo twins;
      Mildred and Anita Secondo
101. Mary Ann and June Borina; Secondo twins
      and their mother
101. June and Mary Ann on lawn (1931)
101. Mary Ann and June Borina (1933)
101. Group at Herbert Ranch (Christmas 1937)
102. Martin, June and Mary Ann Borina with
      horse and wagon (1931)
102. NMB Packing House (1930s)

Credits

C&C. Covello & Covello, Santa Cruz
CT. Cassidy Turley
LT. Land Trust of Santa Cruz County
MR. Mary Rajkovich
PVHA. Pajaro Valley Historical Assn.
RH. Richard Hernandez
RHC. Radović house, Croatia
RP. Sam Vestal, *Register-Pajaronian*
SMB. Sheila McLaughlin Burke
TN. Tom Ninkovich

Bibliography and Sources

Books—
Mekis, Donna F. and Kathryn Mekis Miller. *Blossoms into Gold: The Croatians in the Pajaro Valley*. Capitola, Calif.: Capitola Book Company, 2009.

Ninkovich, Thomas (editor). *The Slav Community of Watsonville, California: As reported in old newspapers (1881-1920)*. Watsonville, Calif.: Reunion Research, 2011.

Prudden, Alyce E. (editor). *A Legal History of Santa Cruz County: An Account of the Local Bench and Bar Through the End of the Twentieth Century*. Santa Cruz, Calif.: Museum of Art & History @ The McPherson Center, 2006.

Author's interviews—
Burke, Sheila, (by telephone), San Mateo Calif., November 19, 2012.
Conti, Samuel (Judge) (by telephone), San Francisco, Calif., August 31, 2012.
Darrow, Robert, Santa Cruz, Calif., July 2007.
Davis, Millie (Secondo) and LuAnn Niebling, Watsonville, Calif., Sept. 27, 2012.
Dobler, Fran, Watsonville, Calif., September 25, 2012.
Ivanovich, John (by telephone), Watsonville, Calif., August 9, 2012.
Kam, Peter (by email), Honolulu, Hawaii, April 19, 2013.
Locke-Paddon, William F., Aptos, Calif., September 5, 2012.
Mekis, Donna F., Santa Cruz, Calif., August 28, 2012.
Moore, Charles, Carmel Valley, Calif., September 18, 2007.
Paxton, Jim, (by telephone), Hollister, Calif., August 2007.
Radin, John, Watsonville, Calif., October 8, 2012.
Radović, Pero (by email), Cavtat, Croatia, February 11, 2013.
Other interviews and conversations were conducted with people who asked not to be quoted by name.

Oral histories, other interviews—
Radovich, Mary Ann (Borina), interviewed in Watsonville by Meri Knaster, June 1977, UC-Santa Cruz Regional Oral History Project.

Schnacke, June (Borina), interviewed by Austin Comstock, June 3, 1999

Stolich, Peter L., and Steve Zupan, interviewed by Zalia Kennedy, April 1987, Pajaro Valley Historical Association – AAUW Oral History Project.

Travers, Ray L., interviewed by Meri Knaster, April 1977, UC-Santa Cruz Regional Oral History Project.

Borina family documents—
Articles of Incorporation of Borina Foundation, filed with California Secretary of State, July 29, 2002.

General ledger, Borina farming operations, 1926-1935, available for inspection at Agricultural History Project, Watsonville.

Handwritten and typed letters between Mary Ann and June Borina, 1938-42; on file with Borina Foundation.

Last Will and Testament of June Borina Schnacke, May 28, 1998.

Newspapers—
Honolulu (HI) *Star-Bulletin*
National Agricultural News (city of origin unknown)
San Francisco (CA) *Chronicle*
San Francisco (CA) *Evening Call*
Santa Cruz (CA) *Penny Press*
Santa Cruz (CA) *Sentinel*
Watsonville (CA) *Evening Pajaronian*
Watsonville (CA) *Register-Pajaronian*

Other periodicals—
The Blue Anchor, publication of the California Fruit Exchange, 1930-35.

"Fruit Markets in Eastern Asia," by B.H. Crocheron and W.J. Norton, *California Agriculture Experiment Station Bulletin #493*, San Francisco, April 1930.

Hastings, published by the University of California, Hastings School of Law, San Francisco. Summer 1996.

Miscellaneous sources—
Vekarić, Nenad (Dr.). "The Filipović/Borina Family." Monograph written for the Borina Foundation, 2004.

Ninkovich, Thomas. "The Filipović/Borina Family." Pamphlet written for the Borina Foundation and based on the above monograph, 2004.

Ninkovich, Thomas. Notes on Borina Family, compiled from private research.

Superior Court, County of Santa Cruz, microfiche records of lawsuits (1925-1960). Read Nov.-Dec. 2012.

U.S. Department of Agriculture, Agricultural Census for California, 1929, 1934.

"An Outline History of Agriculture in the Pajaro Valley," prepared by students in Cabrillo College History 25C, Sandy Lydon, instructor, 1987-88.

"Facts and Figures About the Business of Producing Apples" by Paul S. Williamson, Agricultural Extension Service, Santa Cruz County, 1927.

Agricultural History Project, Watsonville, Apple Exhibit Folder. Read April 2013.

Acknowledgements

The author is first of all grateful to the Borina Foundation for its unstinting support of this project. The book was significantly filled out by many people who were willing to give their time to be interviewed in person, by phone or email: Sheila McLaughlin Burke, Judge Samuel Conti, Robert Darrow, Millie Davis, Fran Dobler, John Ivanovich, Peter Kam, William F. Locke-Paddon, Donna Mekis, Charles Moore, Jr., Luann Niebling, John Radin, Pero Radovich, and numerous others who asked not to be quoted by name. Austin Comstock generously shared his notes on what was, as far as we know, the last interview June Borina ever gave.

Tom Ninkovich did a considerable amount of work on the Borina family line, providing much of the background detail. Sandy Lydon's comments were most valuable in helping establish proper context for the time periods covered by the book. Sheila Prader both helped the author navigate the files at the Agricultural History Project and located some crucial newspaper articles from the 1920s. The Pajaro Valley Historical Association's files were of great help, and Regan Huerta, Jane Borg and Pat Johns went the extra mile to both help locate information and provide leads on matters not in the PVHA archives. Axel Borg and Jeff Hudson helped greatly in sorting the agricultural history files and documents in the UC-Davis collection. Stan Stevens advised on the bibliography and tracked down a critical photograph. The Museum of Art and History in Santa Cruz published this book and lent its facilities and expertise to the storing and selling of it.

The staff and volunteers at the Watsonville and Santa Cruz public libraries went out of their way to be helpful. Linda Sueyoshi at the Hawaii State Library saved a trip across the ocean to run down newspaper files. The staff at the Santa Cruz County Superior Court Clerk's office and at the UC-Santa Cruz Regional History Project were helpful to a fault, making the gathering of detailed information go much more quickly. Jon Covello and Eric Fingal at Covello & Covello Photography were most helpful in locating old photographs and printing them so they looked new.-

Index

About the Author

MIKE WALLACE is a former editor of the Watsonville *Register-Pajaronian*, where he worked for 19 years. Since 1992 he has been a public relations and publications consultant, working with private companies, public agencies and nonprofit organizations. His first mystery novel, *The McHenry Inheritance*, was published by Amazon in 2012. He and his wife, Linda, live in Aptos.